The
SECRET HISTORY
of
CHELMSFORD

The
SECRET HISTORY
of
CHELMSFORD

Paul Wreyford

The
History
Press

This book is dedicated to
Jenny and Rosie

First published 2014

The History Press
The Mill, Brimscombe Port
Stroud, Gloucestershire, GL5 2QG
www.thehistorypress.co.uk

British Library Cataloguing in Publication Data.
A catalogue record for this book is available from the British Library.

ISBN 978 0 7509 5847 9

Typesetting and origination by The History Press
Printed in Great Britain

Contents

Introduction

It is no secret that novelist Charles Dickens once described Chelmsford as 'the dullest and most stupid spot on the face of the earth'. However, he was only a fleeting visitor and never had the time – or perhaps the inclination – to dig a little deeper below the surface.

At first glance, like Dickens, the visitor today might feel England's newest city does not possess much for historians to get excited about. True, Chelmsford is no Colchester. There are no Roman walls and few timber-framed buildings leaning over the high street. But every town and city has a history. In the case of Chelmsford, it is not always visible on the surface and you sometimes have to look a little further to find it.

In fact, Chelmsford – granted city status in 2012 as part of the Queen's Diamond Jubilee celebrations – has a lot to shout about, in historical terms: it was the only place in Britain that Caesar gave his name to, it was briefly the 'capital' of England and it was also the birthplace of radio.

But you know all that already … don't you?

This book does not attempt to tell you what you already know. This book will hopefully tell you the bits you didn't know. Of course, in doing so, I make no apology for touching on Chelmsford's 'famous' events.

However, there are stories surrounding them that have rarely come to light and will be new to most.

Despite the title of this book, I do not claim that the information in the following pages is necessarily a secret. The very word 'secret' means that someone has done their best to conceal something from someone. Most secrets will forever remain so and no digging below the surface will ever reveal them. Having said that, I am confident the majority of the stories and facts on the following pages will be of enlightenment to the average Chelmsfordian.

To be fair to Dickens, it was a dreary Sunday afternoon when he penned those words, gazing out of the window of the now long-gone Black Boy Inn, watching the rain-drops splash into the puddles and wondering when it was going to be dinner time. The only reading material available to him at the time was *Field Exercise and Evolutions of the Army* by Sir Henry Torrens, which he found lying on a sofa. You perhaps cannot blame him for not being too enamoured with the town. However, Essex is a beautiful and undervalued county, and Chelmsford deserves to be the county town and its only city.

I hope this book plays at least a small part in proving that. I would also like to think, should it have been lying on the sofa of the Black Boy Inn that miserable Sunday afternoon, that even the great Charles Dickens himself would have been tempted to pick it up. And by the end of it, one would hope he might have been a little bit more informed and, dare I say it, have even come to a more favourable impression of Chelmsford.

I would like to express my thanks to all those that have helped me with my research, in particular Chelmsford Museum, Essex Record Office, David Taylor, Wendy Hibbitt, Susie Fowkes and Daphne Wreyford. All images are copyright of the author.

Chapter One

Chelmsford
A Brief History
(The bits you probably should already know)

Chelmsford was known as Caesaromagus during Roman times. The name means 'market place of Caesar'. It was the only place in England to bear his name.

The modern name 'Chelmsford' is supposedly derived from an ancient ford called 'Ceolmaer's Ford'. Ceolmaer was a Saxon landowner, the name gradually changing to 'Chelmer' over time.

In about 1100, Maurice, the Bishop of London, fed up with getting his feet wet, built a bridge over the River Can. It meant traffic to and from London was able to cross the river at Ceolmaer's Ford – previously, it had to go via Writtle, then the more important of the two places. The new bridge led to the decline of Writtle but the development of what we now know as Chelmsford.

The high street in Chelmsford – the county town of Essex.

King John granted the Bishop of London the right to hold a weekly market at 'Chelmersford' in 1199. The market brought prosperity and the town grew rapidly. It was not long before it became the county town of Essex.

John soon built a hunting lodge at Writtle, in 1211. John, Henry III and Edward I are among the monarchs said to have stayed there over the years. You can still trace the remains of the royal lodge in the grounds of what is now Writtle College.

Robert the Bruce was reputedly born at Montpelier's Farm, Writtle, in 1274. It is a strong claim and there is plenty of evidence to back it up. The Anglo-Norman family of Bruce owned estates throughout England, one being at Writtle. It is believed the Bruce family obtained the manor of Montpelier via a Norman knight who fought alongside William the Conqueror in 1066.

Moulsham was home to a Dominican friary. It was constructed in the mid-thirteenth century and only demolished by Henry VIII during the Dissolution of the Monasteries. The Mildmay family acquired the site.

Chelmsford became the 'capital' of England for six days in 1381. King Richard II, still a boy at the time, temporarily relocated his government to the town in a bid to restore order following the Peasants' Revolt. The uprising started and finished in Essex, with the last main pocket of resistance suppressed at Norsey Wood on the outskirts of Billericay.

Richard, having gained the upper hand, came to the county town of Essex on 1 July in a bid to reassert his authority. He famously revoked all former pledges he had made to the peasants when they had confronted him at Mile End after marching to London. Frightened Essex rebels, fearing for their lives, came to Chelmsford and pleaded for mercy. The king agreed to spare their lives on the condition that they handed over the ringleaders. Many leaders were taken to the gallows in Chelmsford and executed over the week. The most famous Chelmsford rebel – John Stalworth – was among the ringleaders condemned to die as a traitor. However, Stalworth somehow escaped and fled. He was later granted a pardon under an amnesty and returned to the town to continue his trade as a barber.

Great Baddow also has a claim to playing a part in the revolt. Jack Straw, one of the leaders, is reputed to have rallied the Essex rebels in the churchyard there.

Henry VIII acquired the New Hall estate at Boreham and built a palace, which he named Beaulieu. He wooed Anne Boleyn here but 'imprisoned' daughter Mary Tudor, who later became Mary I, within.

New Hall has been home to many notable people; Oliver Cromwell famously acquired it for just 5s. It is now a prestigious independent school.

King Edward VI Grammar School was founded in 1551 at the dissolved friary, but moved to a new location in Duke Street following the collapse of the classroom in 1627. It relocated to its present location in Broomfield Road in the early 1890s.

Translator Philemon Holland was one of the school's first pupils and arguably the most famous. Holland, who was born in Chelmsford just after the original grammar school opened, was called the 'translator general' of his time.

Thomas Mildmay, a former auditor of the Court of Augmentations, acquired the manors of both Moulsham and Chelmsford in the mid-sixteenth century. The family seat was Moulsham Hall until it was demolished at the beginning of the nineteenth century.

The first execution of a witch in England following a trial in a court of law took place at Chelmsford in the mid-sixteenth century. Agnes Waterhouse was hanged in 1566 after 'confessing' to a number of charges. In 1645, about a dozen supposed witches were hanged at Chelmsford, following another trial in the town. It was the notorious

Thomas Mildmay as depicted on a pub sign.

Witchfinder General Matthew Hopkins who brought them to 'justice'. Essex and Suffolk had the highest number of convictions for witchcraft in England, it being the region in which Hopkins plied his trade.

MP and judge, Sir John Comyns, built Hylands House in about 1730. It was to have many different private owners before Chelmsford Borough Council acquired the estate in the mid-1960s and opened it to the public. Hylands House is still regarded as the jewel in the Chelmsford crown.

The *Chelmsford Chronicle*, one of the oldest weekly newspapers in Britain, was first launched in 1764. It is now known as the *Essex Chronicle*.

The Shire Hall, Chelmsford's most famous building, was built at the design of architect John Johnson in 1791.

The *Essex Chronicle*.

Johnson was responsible for many of the most important buildings that stand in Chelmsford today. He built Stone Bridge over the River Can and was called to repair the roof of what is now the cathedral when it collapsed in 1800.

The Chelmer and Blackwater Navigation opened in 1797. The waterway linked Chelmsford to the sea at

Essex Police HQ.

Maldon and negated the need for goods to be carried on land. It proved a major success. However, the arrival of the railway in Chelmsford in 1843 eventually led to its decline.

Essex Police was formed in 1840. It still has its headquarters in Chelmsford.

A chemist in Tindal Street started to produce and sell flavoured waters in the mid-nineteenth century. His business was to become one of the country's major soft drinks companies, being known as Britvic from 1971.

Chelmsford became a borough in 1888, receiving its charter from Queen Victoria. Architect Fred Chancellor was elected its first mayor.

A public recreation area with sports facilities was created close to the town centre towards the end of the nineteenth century. It is now known as Central Park.

The parish church of St Mary became a cathedral in 1914 when the Diocese of Chelmsford was formed to cover the county of Essex. John Watts-Ditchfield was appointed the first bishop. It is one of the smallest cathedrals in the country.

Chelmsford was home to Britain's first electrical engineering factory. Rookes Evelyn Bell Crompton, a pioneer of electric street lighting, established it. The town was reputedly the first to benefit from this new invention, when Crompton installed electric streetlights to celebrate the incorporation of the Borough of Chelmsford in 1888. However, the council was not sure about the new technology and soon reverted to gas lighting.

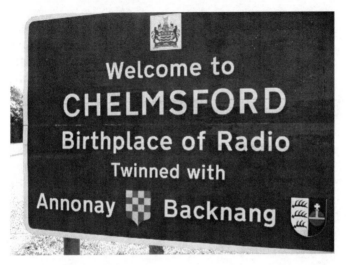

Chelmsford's main claim to fame.

Crompton's firm was one of the 'big three' industries in the town at the beginning of the twentieth century, the other two being Hoffmann and Marconi.

The Hoffmann Manufacturing Company has a place in history for making the 'world go round'. It established the country's first ball bearing factory in Chelmsford. The firm gained worldwide fame for its precision-made bearings.

Chelmsford is the birthplace of radio, as signs inform visitors entering the city. Guglielmo Marconi established the world's first wireless factory in Hall Street in 1899. The company remained there until 1912, when it opened the world's first purpose-built wireless factory in New Street.

It was from New Street, in 1920, that Dame Nellie Melba sang to the world in what was Britain's first official radio broadcast. However, it was Writtle that became the unlikely birthplace of British broadcasting at the beginning of 1922.

The Secret History of Chelmsford

Britain's first regular broadcasting station – 2MT Writtle – operated from a small former army hut in Lawford Lane. It became the catalyst for the BBC, that famous organisation officially registered at the end of the year, many of the Writtle pioneers joining the fledgling company.

Chelmsford became a major target of the German Luftwaffe during the Second World War, due to its major industries. Dozens were killed in one night when a bomb fell close to the Hoffmann factory.

The mayor of Chelmsford, John Ockelford Thompson, was another victim of the air raids. He was killed when a German bomb destroyed his house that stood in what is now New London Road.

Chelmsford became a city in 2012, as part of the Queen's Diamond Jubilee celebrations, and a number of towns battled it out for the honour. Essex, one of the largest counties in England, did not have a city until this time. Rival towns Colchester and Southend were also in the running, but Chelmsford, county town of Essex, won the day. Some might have been forgiven for thinking Chelmsford was already a city, though. It already had a cathedral and the football team has long been known as Chelmsford City FC.

Chapter Two

Chelmsford
A Secret History
(The bits you probably don't already know)

Crime and Punishment

What the Dickens did he Mean?

When Charles Dickens remarked that Chelmsford was 'the dullest and most stupid spot on the face of the earth', he did admit that there were a couple of things worth seeing in the town.

However, they are hardly the places tourism bosses of the day would have been at great pains to point out. It was not the cathedral or the impressive Shire Hall that Dickens was referring to – but the prison ... or both of them, to be precise!

Dickens, who came to Chelmsford as a newspaper reporter in 1835, staying at the Black Boy Inn, observed that the only things to look at were not one, but two 'immense prisons large enough to hold all the inhabitants of the county'. Indeed, there can have been few places in Britain that once had two gaols in simultaneous use.

The original prison, known as Moulsham Gaol, was built on the south bank of the River Can during the mid-seventeenth century. It stood overlooking the bridge that still connects Moulsham to Chelmsford, but there is no trace of it today. Indeed, the first prison only lasted some 100 years. It was demolished and rebuilt in 1777, the year after several prisoners escaped by lifting up the floor-boards and digging a tunnel to reach the adjoining yard.

Like most prisons of the time, conditions were very poor. Lack of adequate manpower meant that the inmates were forced to spend day and night locked in their cells for fear they would attempt to make their escape. As a result, typhus or 'gaol fever' was a common problem.

Moulsham Gaol was situated next to Stone Bridge on the south bank of the river.

There were many prisoners in each cell and very little in the way of ventilation. Security did not seem to improve and not even confining inmates to their cells could prevent the very determined escaping. In 1817, eleven prisoners made their escape via the sewers, though all were later recaptured. It is believed they got out by descending into a sewer via the privy in their cell.

More alterations were made to the prison in 1819, but it was eventually decided to build a new gaol at Springfield, the one that is familiar to Chelmsfordians today.

The new prison at Springfield was built between 1822 and 1828. However, what is not so widely known is that Moulsham Gaol did not close immediately and, when Dickens came to town, both old and new prisons were in use. In fact, the original prison was still being used as late as 1848. That we know because of an unfortunate woman known as Mary May. She was the first woman to be hanged at the new Springfield prison. However, following her conviction for killing her half-brother, she was accommodated at Moulsham. She was only transferred to Springfield a couple of nights before her execution in 1848. Some 3,000 people witnessed her demise. However, with public executions being the entertainment of the day, there was nothing unusual about that.

Local 'Hero'

It is perhaps fitting that the most famous executioner of the nineteenth century should sometimes ply his trade in the new prison at Springfield. However, most Chelmsford residents today would not have the faintest idea why that should be. Indeed, few know that William Calcraft – not only the most famous hangman of his time but also the most notorious – was a local man.

Perhaps that is not surprising. Calcraft was hardly a hero of the town and his occupation was not something that brought a lot of honour to Chelmsford. Needless to say, as far as I am aware, no blue plaque is currently in the pipeline.

However, Calcraft, who was born just outside Chelmsford in the village of Little Baddow, would have known the town very well – particularly the bit within the walls of the new gaol. Of course, it was not his chief place of work. That was the infamous Newgate Prison. However, Calcraft travelled throughout the country to carry out hangings and Chelmsford was one of his many ports of call.

Calcraft may not be very familiar to residents today, but he was almost a celebrity in his time. Charles Dickens, who campaigned vigorously against capital punishment, certainly knew him and was less than impressed with his persona. He wrote that Calcraft should refrain from drinking brandy and telling jokes on the scaffold! It is unlikely Dickens got the opportunity to witness an execution at Springfield, however, but thousands did.

Happily for Dickens, executions in public were finally banned in 1868. It was Calcraft himself that carried out both the last public execution in Britain and the first to be held in private. It is thought that Calcraft carried out between 400 and 500 executions before his retirement in 1874. He was one of Britain's longest-serving executioners, but is often referred to as one of the most incompetent. It is said he frequently failed to calculate the correct length of rope – he was known on occasions to have to rush below the scaffold and pull on the legs of the victim to complete the job.

Calcraft could make a lot of money from his occupation. Not only did he receive payment for carrying out an execution, but he would also benefit from selling memorabilia, such as pieces of the rope. This was particularly the case should the condemned criminal have been something of

The current prison at Springfield.

a celebrity. Calcraft – as hangman – was also entitled to the victim's personal belongings. Madame Tussaud would sometimes buy the clothes from him in order to dress the newly commissioned waxwork of the victim that would soon be displayed in her Chamber of Horrors.

A Jailer or Two That Ended Up the Wrong Side of the Bars

It is probably safe to assume that people were not exactly queuing up to become a gaoler in days gone by. It was not the most desirable job. The original prison at Moulsham was not a pretty place to work. And yet it could be a profitable one.

William Cawthorn seemed to do quite well until his activities were brought to light. Cawthorn (the derivative spelling of the surname) was the keeper of the House of Correction at Moulsham Gaol, when magistrates carried out an investigation into his affairs in 1822.

He was accused of a number of offences, including receiving illegal payments for the release of prisoners.

Of course, he would not have been the only corrupt jailer of his time. Gaolers could supplement their modest income by accepting bribes, and many did. In fact, the practice of prison workers taking payments of various kinds from inmates had reached such heights during the first part of the nineteenth century that an Act had to be introduced in 1815 to make it illegal.

However, Cawthorn may have taken things a bit too far. He was accused of the unnecessary flogging of prisoners, and fixing chains or weights to their legs in order to increase the suffering. Cawthorn was also suspected of attempting to rape a debtor. He would not have been a very popular figure and there is every possibility the charges were exaggerated or even made up by those who had a personal vendetta against him, though he is certainly said to have been negligent, rude and sometimes violent, at the very least.

Mrs Cawthorn and John Wood, their nephew, were also brought to book by the authorities. There are some who say that Wood was the man really in charge of the House of Correction at Moulsham, it obviously being a family-run business at the time. Cawthorn kept no accounts. Wood is said to have taken responsibility for that, no doubt at his own choosing.

Criminal proceedings were commenced against the trio and another turnkey. Ironically, it is believed Wood absconded and left his partners in crime to face the music. It is said that both Mr and Mrs Cawthorn found themselves behind bars for a spell. However, there are also reports that Mr Cawthorn himself somehow did a runner and avoided trial. Certainly, by 1823, a reward was being offered for his apprehension. If that is so, he did not appear to take Mrs Cawthorn with him. According to records, she was sentenced and jailed for her part in the prison scandal. One can only hope, for her sake, that her gaoler had been a little bit more sensitive towards her.

With Cawthorn locked up – or on the run, whichever story you wish to believe – a new keeper was required. The job was eventually handed to Thomas Clarkson Neale. And, while still holding this office, he was famously also appointed the first governor of the new gaol at Springfield.

'Nosy' Parker Taught Prisoners a Lesson

Not all jailers at the old Moulsham Gaol were unforgiving brutes. In fact, one keeper, named Mr Parker, certainly appeared to be ahead of his time when it came to prison reform.

At the beginning of the nineteenth century, some prisoners were plotting to make their escape. Mr Parker had ensured he had a good intelligence system operating within the cells and he discovered the conspiracy before it was too late. The culprits must have feared the worst. At best, they would be subjected to a severe beating. However, Mr Parker took a different route. He thought long and hard over how he could teach the offenders a lesson.

His solution was a novel one. On Christmas Day he provided a special dinner within the walls of the prison. It was for all the prisoners to enjoy – with the exception of those who had conspired to make their escape. According to a newspaper report, they 'were put upon the long chain and stationed off the tables when their fellow prisoners were enjoying a hearty meal of beef and soup, of which they were only suffered to enjoy the smell'.

Gaols and Goals

Imposing Chelmsford Prison – the name used for the gaol at Springfield today – appears to have little in common with a top football club. And Craven Cottage – the home of Fulham FC – is also a far cry from that particular establishment, even if long-suffering FFC fans (including the author of this book) may have on occasions likened the experience of watching their team to that of serving a prison sentence.

The connection between the two is a man named Thomas Hopper. As an architect, he made his name in 1806 when he redesigned the original Craven Cottage, the property that stood on the site now occupied by the football club and after which the present stadium is named. His work on Craven Cottage resulted in a commission from no less than the Prince Regent, who asked him to transform Carlton House. It was the break he needed and the reputation of Hopper grew.

However, Hopper – despite his growing portfolio – was never commissioned to design a public building, once considered to be the ultimate compliment shown to an architect. That changed when Hopper was appointed

There is a connection between Chelmsford Prison and a top football club.

surveyor to the county of Essex and the job of designing the new gaol at Springfield was handed to him. It became his one and only public building.

The Great Escapes

Chelmsford Prison – like its predecessor at Moulsham – has witnessed many, mostly unsuccessful, bids for freedom over the years. Some escapes have been planned, while other prisoners have just seized the moment.

William Cooper was the first convict to escape from the new prison, about a year after it was opened. He was responsible for lighting the lamps and was allowed, under supervision, a ladder for the purpose. That ladder was left unattended in the prison yard on one occasion and Cooper was unable to resist the temptation. He was not seen again for about a year, when one of his Chelmsford prison officers recognised him at Ipswich Gaol, where he was being detained in connection with a robbery.

You have to admire the gall of another prisoner who escaped in the early 1830s. It was not so much his escape that is memorable, but the fact that, two nights later, he parcelled up his prison clothes and threw them back over the prison wall. It is said he did not want to take the risk of being prosecuted for stealing them.

One of the biggest breaks for freedom occurred in 1837. The surgeon was called in when one of the prisoners pretended to be ill. The warder escorting the surgeon was set upon by a large group of prisoners and had his keys taken from him. The prisoners took flight, using the keys to access other parts of the prison, releasing more inmates as they went. Guards eventually thwarted them, though they got as far as charging the side gate. Even if they had managed to penetrate the gate, it is unlikely they would have got far. It seems community spirit was strong in Chelmsford at that particular time,

The high walls of Chelmsford Prison have not always been successful in keeping prisoners in.

as residents, aware there was a disturbance within the walls of the prison, gallantly surrounded the establishment. A press report at the time stated: 'Great praise is due to the officers for their alertness, their courage, and their coolness of temper; and the prompt attendance of at least 500 of the inhabitants of Chelmsford, who surrounded the prison on the first alarm, to prevent the escape of any of the prisoners over the wall, might have been of the greatest assistance.'

Of course, the most famous 'escape' appeared on the big screen. Chelmsford Prison was the setting for the film version of the hit television series *Porridge*, starring Ronnie Barker.

That the film was shot there is no secret, but people have often wondered what the authorities did with the real prisoners. Sad to say, they were not used as extras. The prison was empty at the time. The current inmates had to be rehomed for a spell following a major fire in

1978, and the Home Office gave the film crew special permission to use the empty building. It had previously refused to allow the TV series to be shot in a real prison, as the producers had hoped.

Some of the actual cells were used during filming and prison officers were on hand to offer their expertise to the producers. Apparently, the prison officers 'treated' the film crew to a meal when filming was completed, dishing up – you guessed it – porridge!

Final Fling

The final execution to take place in Chelmsford occurred towards the end of 1914.

The hanging of Charles Frembd also has a place in history, for he was the oldest man to be hanged in Britain in the twentieth century. He was 71.

Hangman John Ellis executed the German-born grocer from Leytonstone at the new Springfield Prison. He had been convicted of murdering his wife. However, he claimed that he did the deed under severe provocation. Mrs Frembd was found lying in bed with her throat cut. Her husband was found beside her with a self-inflicted cut to the throat, though his injury was a minor one and he lived to tell the tale.

However, if Frembd had not survived his suicide attempt, he had also conveniently left a note in which he gave the reasons for his actions. The note explained that Mrs Frembd's first husband had 'made off with himself' and Frembd added that he too felt unable to live in her presence any longer. He penned: 'God forgive me. Her temper done it.'

The School Saint

Few people not associated with St John Payne Catholic School will know how that particular establishment got its name.

The Secret History of Chelmsford

John Payne, a saint of the Roman Catholic Church, was a priest who met his fate at Chelmsford in 1582. Payne was the only Catholic priest to be executed in Essex during the reign of Queen Elizabeth I. Of course, many more Protestants had suffered the same fate under Queen Mary I, including Thomas Watts, who was burnt at the stake in 1555. A plaque near Stone Bridge marks the spot where Watts spent his final few hours.

Another to be executed at Chelmsford was George 'Trudgeover' Eagles. He earned his nickname by travelling from place to place to preach Protestantism, something that would not have pleased 'Bloody Mary', who made restoring Catholicism the main aim of her reign. The horrific punishment of Eagles is no secret, the preacher being hanged, drawn and quartered. His body was divided into four parts, one quarter being displayed at Chelmsford, the others throughout Essex. His head was placed on a long pole and exhibited on the market cross until the wind blew it down. It lay on the ground for several days until someone had the decency, or courage, to bury it in the churchyard.

The execution of gentle John Payne, also sentenced to suffer the death of a traitor, might have been just as horrific. However, the crowd, such was their sympathy for the priest, begged the hangman to allow men to hang on the feet of the condemned in order to ensure he was dead before being quartered, and thus prevent him from any further suffering.

Payne was held in high regard, and not only within Catholic circles. Most were of the opinion he was innocent of the charges laid upon him. Payne, for many years, resided at nearby Ingatestone Hall in the guise of an estate steward. The owner of the house – the Catholic Lady Petre – harboured many seminary priests. It was not a good time to be a practising Catholic and Payne was forced to conduct services in secret. He was betrayed by a spy named George Eliot, an apostate Catholic, who had been a servant at Ingatestone Hall. A trumped-up charge of plotting to dethrone Elizabeth was laid before Payne. It appears only the court believed Eliot's claim that Payne had uttered treasonable words while at Ingatestone.

The courageous priest suffered much before his execution. He spent some eight months being tortured in the Tower of London, but he would not recant his faith and conform to the new Church of England. On the scaffold he continued to declare that 'his feet did never tread, his hands did never write, nor his wit ever invent any treason against Her Majesty'. Indeed, most believed him. It appears this sincere man had only ever wanted to worship God in the way he chose.

Payne was canonised in 1970 and at least now has a fitting memorial in Chelmsford, thanks to the city's Roman Catholic secondary school.

'Fowl' Play Led to Further Tragedy

Two innocent men once died for the sake of a pheasant or two.

A terrible murder in the mid-nineteenth century – bad enough in its own right – was to lead to the death of a second innocent person in quite tragic and unusual circumstances.

At St Andrew's church in Boreham, you will find the tombstone of William Hales, gamekeeper to Sir John Tyrell of Boreham House. Hales was only in his early forties when he was shot and killed by poachers on 19 February 1856. The gamekeeper had confronted a group of men shooting pheasants on the land of his employer. When he attempted to intervene, a gun was turned on him. The incident shocked Chelmsford.

Hales left a large family, and neighbours rallied round to provide for his widow and children, collecting a substantial amount of money for their future upkeep.

So many people wanted to see that justice was done that, when the accused poachers appeared in court

The grave of William Hales.

at the Shire Hall in Chelmsford, the premises proved wholly inadequate. The trial was to take place in an upper courtroom, but it was not big enough to accommodate the huge crowd that had gathered. It resulted in lots of people congregating on the staircase, all attempting to gain admittance to the room itself. Sadly, the staircase could not take their weight and collapsed. A young man named Moss died. He could only be identified by his watch, his face having been so mutilated during the crush.

The collapse caused a large gap between the stairs and courtroom, effectively stranding all those already in the room, including the defendants. All had to exit the building through the windows, via ladders that were placed in the adjoining churchyard of St Mary's church, now the city cathedral. For many years, curious sightseers were shown the bloodstains on the floor marking the spot where poor Mr Moss had fallen.

The poachers did not escape justice, however. Though the man who fired the gun escaped the death penalty, he and his accomplices were transported to Australia to serve a varying number of years in hard labour.

That is not quite the end of the story, for there was to be an incredible twist in the tale. It has been said in these parts that one of the daughters of Mr Hales (some say it was actually his widow) was travelling on a train from London to Chelmsford several years after the incident. Some men in the carriage, unaware who she might be, asked her if she could recall a day when the stairs at the Shire Hall collapsed during a trial. She nodded and explained that the trial was for the murder of her father. The men then replied it was they who had been on trial on that fateful day. They were at that very moment returning home, having served their sentences in Australia.

Health and Education

He Didn't Spread It Around

If you had examined the parish burial register in the second half of the seventeenth century you might have been forgiven for thinking Moulsham got off lightly when the Great Plague struck in 1665–66: only one burial of a known victim was recorded. However, there is thought to have been about 500 victims in Chelmsford and Moulsham, which at the time would have been about a quarter of the population.

It is not known why the burial of Moulsham man John Spight was the only one of a plague victim to be recorded in the parish burial register. It could be that he just happened to be the first of many to succumb to the disease. It is therefore presumed that so many deaths followed, it was deemed a futile task to keep up with proceedings. Of course, it is just as probable that the residents of the time were too preoccupied to care about keeping records up to date. The words 'plague time' were penned in the margin in 1666 and are probably a sufficient explanation.

The plague started in London and soon spread to Essex, many Londoners fleeing to neighbouring counties in a bid to escape it. Those that fled may have already been infected, though travellers and tradesmen have also been blamed for bringing it to Chelmsford. How exactly it got to Chelmsford will never be known, but Spight, it appears, was to become the town's first unlucky victim. He died in August 1665. At the time, a man named John Green was the Overseer of the Poor in Moulsham. He recorded the death of Spight in his own accounts. That Spight was the first of many to fall victim to the plague is highlighted by a note Green also penned, referring to his death as 'ye beginning of ye visitation'.

The Great Plague was confined to Moulsham at first.

The Overseers of the Poor in neighbouring Chelmsford, just across the river, decided Green should have sole responsibility in ensuring the plague did not reach their domain. Green revealed in his own records that he was promised a payment of £5 to keep the infection from spreading beyond Moulsham. He would have required plenty of money. The quarantined sick needed to be nursed and supported; gravediggers had to be paid and rewards offered to those willing to bear the bodies to their final place of rest.

The doors of houses of a known victim were secured. Infected families were effectively imprisoned in their own homes. The watchman was provided with shot and powder to prevent any occupant from leaving an infected home and spreading the disease. It must have been a terrifying time.

The infection did not reach Chelmsford until the spring of 1666. Green had succeeded in preventing it from spreading from Moulsham for almost nine months, no mean feat. It is perhaps no wonder he did not have time or the inclination to record the names of those that had fallen victim to it.

Serve Yourself

Whole families in Chelmsford were wiped out by the plague. However, one story to emerge from the plague of 1637 backs up the old adage that one man's loss is another man's gain, or in this case, a woman's gain.

That particular woman – a servant – appeared to benefit from the demise of the Hull family. She watched the whole household fall victim to the infection. Within the space of a few weeks, Mr and Mrs Hull, plus their daughter, all succumbed to the plague. It left the servant alone in the house.

The executors of the will of Thomas Hull, for fear of becoming infected themselves, refused to go into the house to arrange the affairs of the family. They positioned themselves at a fair distance away from the property one day and called out to the servant. She was told to come outside and, from the safety of the other side of the fence, they conducted their business. She was paid her wages (presumably the money was thrown over the fence in an envelope) and the servant was instructed to stay in the house for a set amount of time, as people would be fearful of catching the infection from her. She was given permission to consume the food and ale in the house that belonged to her master. And it appears she helped herself to a bit more than that. One resident is said to have seen the servant's sister pick up a piece of silver from the street that had been thrown from an open window on one occasion. When she finally emerged from the house – having herself somehow escaped becoming infected – the servant was said to be carrying a number of boxes. Her 'belongings' deemed to be far greater than that which a humble person in service would normally have in their possession.

Doctor Who?

It is perhaps something of a mystery as to why the name of eighteenth-century surgeon Benjamin Pugh is not hailed from the rooftops in Chelmsford. It has to be said that few today have even heard of him.

And yet one might put forward the case that no other former resident of the town, throughout its long history, saved as many Chelmsford lives as Dr Pugh did during his lifetime.

Pugh was a pioneer in at least two fields – midwifery and the inoculation of smallpox. It is safe to say that he saved many through his expertise and inventiveness.

Midwifery in the mid-eighteenth century was still the realm of women and not even considered a particularly important field within medical circles. Pugh, in his *Treatise of Midwifery* (published in 1754), attempted to change that. He penned: 'Don't think because midwifery has been hitherto chiefly in the hands of women, that it is a trifling affair; very far from it, be assured.'

Mothers and babies died during delivery at an alarming rate. It was almost accepted and not challenged. Pugh came up with some pioneering tools and methods to stem the flow of 'unnecessary' deaths. The first description of an endotracheal tube can be found in Pugh's treatise. At the time it was known simply as 'Pugh's pipe'. The pipe was described as being 10in long and able to be inserted through the windpipe of the baby as far as the larynx. Bellows could be attached to it in order to inflate the lungs. Its aim was to provide an airway to babies during obstructed labour.

Pugh also invented his own forceps and used mouth-to-mouth resuscitation on babies, something not as common as it is today. His treatise contains advice on what to do should the baby not be breathing upon delivery. He wrote: 'Wipe its mouth, and press your mouth to the child's, at the same time pinching the nose with your thumb and finger, to prevent the air escaping; inflate the lungs; rubbing it before the fire; by which method I have saved many.'

In the treatise, Pugh estimated that he had delivered about 2,000 babies. He had some novel approaches to childbirth, also being of the opinion that the mother should be discouraged from lying down when giving birth, an idea many choose to adopt today, though at the time it would have been a radical suggestion. He also advised surgeons that it would be helpful if they remained sober throughout!

Smallpox was another big problem in Chelmsford in the mid-eighteenth century. Many lost their lives to the disease. Pugh claimed to be one of the first inoculators against smallpox in England.

Pugh built a grand property in the high street known as Mansion House. It appears he was deserving of it. We shall, of course, never know just how many lives Dr Pugh did save, but we can be sure many owed their life to him. When statues have been erected to much less worthier individuals, it is perhaps a little sad this humane and innovative medical man remains unknown to the average Chelmsfordian of today.

Pen and (Dr)ink

It is perhaps ironic that the former home of writer Oliver Goldsmith should today stand in the shadow of a private hospital.

Many have checked in at the Priory Hospital in Springfield Green in order to be treated for alcohol addiction among other things. And Goldsmith could have done himself some good if he had done likewise. Of course, the well-known hospital never existed in his day and it is unlikely the novelist, playwright and poet would have sought help in any case.

It is no secret that Goldsmith once resided in what is now Dukes Cottages (opposite the parish church) towards the end of his life for a brief period, during which time he is said to have penned 'The Deserted Village', one of the most famous and most quoted poems in English literature.

However, what is not so well known is that Goldsmith's time at Chelmsford would probably not have been his happiest, at least as far as his health was concerned. Goldsmith's body broke down in his later years, due mainly to his love of drink. Despite his ailing health, Goldsmith chose to treat himself, rejecting the assistance of medical professionals, preferring to accept the advice of indifferent chemists. Dr Samuel Johnson famously said of Goldsmith: 'No man was more foolish when he had not a pen in his hand, or more wise when he had.'

Not helped by mounting debts, the vain and sensitive Goldsmith died a broken man in 1774. It has often been said he lived too hard and drank too much. He was only in his early forties.

The former home of Oliver Goldsmith.

It has been suggested that 'Sweet Auburn' in 'The Deserted Village' was inspired by Springfield. It has to be said most are of the opinion that Goldsmith was thinking of his own village in his native Ireland when penning the work. However, others suggest that parts of the poem, particularly the description of the church, do indeed refer to Springfield.

The poem laments the decline of village life and is a melancholy piece, though one could be forgiven for thinking that Goldsmith might not have only been referring to his changing surroundings, but his own fading health and general decline: 'Thy sports are fled, and all thy charms withdrawn; Amidst thy bowers the tyrant's hand is seen, And desolation saddens all thy green.'

The First 'Health and Safety Officer'

There are few in cosseted Britain today who are not of the opinion that 'health and safety' has gone a little bit too far these days. Most of us just groan when we read reports in our newspapers of schools forbidding conker fights, or the banning of pins to secure poppies. However, stories like these are, in fact, nothing new.

By the end of the nineteenth century, Chelmsford already had a 'health and safety officer'. The first was Edward Hunt Carter. He took up his position in 1872, his real job title being Medical Officer of Health to Chelmsford's local board. Unlike many ridiculed health and safety officers in big companies today – who are often viewed as someone merely out to spoil everyone's fun – Carter, it appears, was a very popular man, full of practical advice for the public.

However, the prevention of accidents was one aspect of his role that he took very seriously. It may have been getting on for 150 years ago, but Carter was nevertheless bemoaning the fact that boys were using icy pavements as slides, and was also alluding to the fact that the general public was in danger because of the 'great number of children who daily infest the public streets and there amuse themselves with tops and other children's toys'. Sadly, it is not known just how many unwary pedestrians succumbed to a spinning top or two.

To be fair to Carter, he achieved much of far greater importance in his role. He lived at a time when the health and safety of the public was of great concern. With smallpox and other diseases rife, he called for an isolation hospital and was also successful in establishing a mortuary in the town. He wisely pointed out the fact that keeping a dead body in the house until burial, often for more than a few days, was not the best idea. In 1882, the authorities purchased one of the railway arches in Viaduct Road from the railway company, the premises becoming the first public mortuary in Chelmsford.

He Should Have Listened to the Teacher

It was deemed a miracle that no one was hurt when the classroom roof came down at the free grammar school in 1627. Fortunately, the children were at lunch. If they had been at study, it is likely few would have survived.

The incident is no secret. However, few will know that a former master predicted it some twenty-five years earlier.

Thomas Mildmay, a former auditor of the Court of Augmentations, founded the free grammar school in 1551 in one of the few surviving halls of the former friary at Moulsham, which was demolished during the Dissolution of the Monasteries. Following his death, his son, also called Thomas, managed the affairs of the school, though, according to schoolmaster Richard Broadway, not very well.

It is highly likely that the building was in a poor condition even when the Mildmays obtained it. Over the years it would have got worse. Broadway accused the new Thomas Mildmay of neglecting it. The situation got so bad that Broadway dipped into his own pocket in order to carry out repairs, lest 'it should fall down, being very ruinous'.

Broadway had many other complaints and it is safe to say he was not the greatest friend of Mildmay. The Mildmays were the most important family in Chelmsford and one should perhaps admire the courage and determination of Broadway in taking them on. When Mildmay and his fellow governors refused to take action over his many complaints, particularly the state of the building, Broadway eventually petitioned the king himself – James I – in 1605. An inquiry took place in the following year, but little

The present King Edward VI Grammar School.

seems to have been resolved before both Mildmay and Broadway died a few years later. And, it appears the warning of Broadway went unheeded in the years to follow as well, as the school did fall down, just as Broadway had predicted.

The building was deemed to be beyond repair following the incident and the school was moved to new premises in Duke Street. It left that site in the early 1890s and relocated to its present home in Broomfield Road. The King Edward VI Grammar School, today known to most Chelmsfordians as KEGS, now has a fine reputation and, needless to say, a strong roof.

The Forgotten Student Who Asked Us to Remember

'We will remember them.'

So wrote poet Laurence Binyon. And, of course, we do remember fallen soldiers during gatherings at war memorials up and down the country every November. However, not a lot of people remember Laurence Binyon, or at least his time in Chelmsford. It is not widely advertised that Binyon was once a resident in the town.

He came to Chelmsford as a young boy after his father, Frederick, was appointed curate at St Mary's church in 1874. He held that position until 1878, during which time the young Laurence, who was born in 1869, briefly attended King Edward VI Grammar School, then situated in Duke Street.

Even biographical accounts of Binyon often omit his Chelmsford years and most residents today are oblivious to the fact that one of our great poets was partly educated here. Binyon may not have gained immortality in Chelmsford, but his poem 'For the Fallen' – thanks to the poignant lines of the fourth verse – certainly has, being read at Remembrance Sunday ceremonies throughout the world.

Let's Drink to That!

Writtle College – now producing the country's leading agriculturists and horticulturists, among other things – has a fine reputation that has spread well beyond Chelmsford. Television celebrity Alan Titchmarsh is a patron and its success is no secret.

It would be fitting to raise a glass to celebrate the success of any similar establishment. However, in the case of Writtle College, it is particularly fitting to raise a glass or two. In fact, it is a good job people did enjoy a tipple in moralistic Victorian England. Not many people know that Writtle College – though it has not always been known by that name – came into being thanks to Britain's love of alcohol.

Drunkenness was a big problem in Victorian times. The working class, many forced to endure poor living conditions, saw alcohol as an escape. Parliament was of the opinion that the humble public house was partly responsible for tempting people to drink too much. Politicians felt there were now too many pubs and decided to revoke a number of licences in order to remove the 'temptation' from the streets.

That was not the only step taken. In the early 1890s, a liquor tax was slapped on the sale of alcohol in a further bid to clean up the streets. No doubt fearing the act would be deemed as being just another way for the government to make money, politicians decided that all the revenue from the tax would be used as compensation for the publicans who had had their licences revoked. However, most of the pub owners affected were large breweries. Already very wealthy, they did not need extra money for closing one or two of their pubs, which to them was like a drop in the ocean. The public was furious with the idea that they would have to pay tax on their alcohol, knowing the money would be going to rich breweries. Their protests forced the

Writtle College.

government to come up with another idea. Parliament was in a quandary, however. The country had already raised a substantial amount of money from the liquor tax, but now did not know what to do with it.

Eventually, it was decided to spend the surplus money on technical education. Essex County Council came to the decision that it would spend its share of the 'whisky money', as it became known, on purchasing the former King Edward VI Grammar School buildings on Duke Street for the purpose of providing technical training in agriculture and horticulture. And so, in 1893, Writtle College was born.

Writtle College has been known by many names and, of course, did not gain its current one until moving to that particular village on the outskirts of Chelmsford when a local farmer offered his estate for sale. It is perhaps the right name, though 'Whisky College' would have been a more interesting one.

The 'Art' and Soul of University

It has to be said that many Chelmsfordians have no idea how the city's university got its name.

The Anglia Ruskin University is, of course, named after Victorian art critic and social reformer John Ruskin, the Anglia prefix explaining that there are now three campuses in the region: at Cambridge, Peterborough and Chelmsford.

However, the university might have been known by a different name and it is perhaps something of a disservice to Revd William John Beamont that it does not bear his. Many Chelmsford residents wrongly, but perhaps not surprisingly, believe Ruskin was the founder of the establishment. It was, in fact, Beamont, a humble clergyman. And while Ruskin is remembered as an eminent Victorian, a man of the people, Revd Beamont is all but forgotten today. However, the two were very similar. Revd Beamont was a man who, like Ruskin, had a passion for art and education. Beamont was himself fortunate to enjoy an education at Eton and Cambridge. However, he knew others were not so lucky and, during a spell as a curate in London and then as a vicar in Cambridge, Beamont worked hard for the working classes. Like Ruskin, social reform was high on his agenda.

Beamont founded the Cambridge School of Art in 1858, which later became the Cambridgeshire College of Arts and Technology. This college merged with the existing Essex Institute of Higher Education and the new establishment eventually became known as Anglia Polytechnic University in the early 1990s. Having gained university status, the 'polytechnic' was dropped and a new name was sought.

It was Ruskin who delivered the inaugural speech when the Cambridge School of Art opened back in the mid-nineteenth century. He was the perfect choice for the task. His passion for art and social reform was to inspire a generation, from politicians and philosophers, to artists and writers. Gandhi, Tolstoy and Oscar Wilde are among those who were influenced by the ideas of John Ruskin.

Sadly for Beamont, he never had the chance to achieve the fame of his like-minded contemporary. The clergyman was only 40 when he died in 1868. Ruskin made it to the twentieth century.

One can quite understand why the name Ruskin was chosen for the prestigious seat of learning that now sits at the heart of Chelmsford, but you cannot help but feel the 'Anglia Beamont University' would have done just as well.

Another Man Who Should Have Made a Name for Himself

Many might know that a Chelmsford man was responsible for founding a college of Cambridge University. However, it is less widely known that he was not the only Chelmsfordian to do so.

Sir Walter Mildmay – a member of the most important family in Chelmsford for many centuries – founded Emmanuel College. It became a famous seat of learning for Puritans, with preacher Thomas Hooker among its former pupils. It is not surprising that Mildmay should be remembered in history, having also risen to become Chancellor of the Exchequer. He was just one of a number of prominent Mildmays.

However, Walter Mildmay was not the first Chelmsford man to leave his mark on Cambridge.

Richard de Baddow was born, as his name suggests, at Great Baddow. He was himself educated at Cambridge and became chancellor of the university in 1326. In that year he purchased two houses that he subsequently handed over to the university. They were to form a new college that was named University Hall.

Ironically, it was not at first successful and attracted few scholars. So, in 1338, Richard de Baddow assigned all the rights and titles to Elizabeth de Clare, the grand-daughter of Edward I. She refounded the college and gave it a new name.

Clare College is a name now known throughout the world. However, if things had been a little different, it might have been 'Baddow' College that students from all over are now aspiring to attend.

Something 'Cropped' Up On My Way Home

Agricultural workers of the last century should probably be thankful that Henry Ford was travelling by train and not in one of his reliable cars on one memorable day in 1930.

The automobile manufacturer was returning from Harwich, having been in Europe, when his train was held up just before reaching Chelmsford. If it had not

Boreham House caught the eye of Henry Ford.

been held up for a few minutes, he would probably not have noticed Boreham House sitting in the distance across the fields. At the time, the property was in a poor condition and the whole estate was for sale. Ford was surprised to see so many dilapidated farm buildings in the Essex countryside. He was told that the reason was because poor wages were prompting more and more agricultural workers to look for employment in urban areas. Youngsters no longer wanted to be farmers. He was shocked.

Ford, though he made his name manufacturing cars, was the son of a farmer and farming remained in his blood. He was horrified to learn that British agriculture was no longer a prosperous business and was in decline. He set about changing that.

Ford decided to buy Boreham House and its surrounding land. He never intended to personally live in the mansion. It was the entire estate that had attracted him, believing it to be the ideal location for a college. Ford subsequently established the Henry Ford Institute of Agricultural Engineering. The seat of learning was to provide courses in the agriculture industry for farmers and farm workers. It was the first of its kind in the country.

Ford had revolutionary ideas. He was convinced higher wages could be paid if there was better managing or marketing. And he was keen to ensure those responsible for producing the food we ate should enjoy a greater share of the financial harvest.

Ford died in 1947. He had started to make agricultural machinery long before he made his first car. And it was to this first love he returned after he had made his fortune. While it is nearby Dagenham that will forever be linked with the name of Ford, Chelmsford – thanks to a late-running train – has at least something to shout about in the success story of one of America's most famous sons.

Religion and Politics

Grave Times

Clergymen conducting a burial do not expect to end up in the grave with the corpse. Unfortunately, that was exactly what happened to a former rector of Chelmsford Cathedral, then St Mary's church.

Poor John Michaelson was rector at the wrong time. He served the town during a period when the country was in religious and political turmoil. The English Civil War had just started and the Parliamentarians, having seized control, did not like the fact that Michaelson – under his superiors' orders – was still using the Book of Common Prayer during burial services. The angry soldiers interrupted the proceedings at the graveside and threw the unfortunate rector and the offending book into the open grave with the corpse. They then started to fill in the grave with earth, intent on burying Michaelson alive. He was only saved by some of his parishioners.

It was not the first or last time Michaelson was assaulted by the Parliamentarians. However, it is ironic that he should suffer so much at their hands. In fact, he often caused the consternation of his own side. Michaelson, though a Church of England clergyman, had leanings towards Puritanism himself. He served at the same time famous Puritan Thomas Hooker was lecturer at St Mary's, and it is said the two got on well. Michaelson actively encouraged the controversial Hooker, who caused outrage among followers of the established church. He stood by Hooker until the day the latter was hounded out of Chelmsford in about 1630. It seems that Hooker acted as almost like a curate to Michaelson. Under pressure from the Bishop of London, William Laud, and other influential Church of England men to conform, Michaelson apparently eventually did so and, unlike Hooker, managed to retain his position at St Mary's, at least for a few more years.

However, many still did not trust him and he had to be rebuked for his occasional non-conformism, which included only turning up for the service once preliminary prayers had concluded (Michaelson was uncomfortable with the compulsory use of the Book of Common Prayer). It is therefore something of an injustice that Michaelson should have been the target of so much hatred from non-conformists. Clearly, Michaelson had sympathy with their objection to the idolatry and superstitions of the Church.

In 1641, extremists used poles to smash the east window of St Mary's church. The window only contained plain glass, the churchwardens – at the order of the Parliamentarians – having already removed the original glass depicting images of the Virgin Mary and Christ which would have so offended the Puritans. However, the mob that had gathered in the churchyard that night were still angered by the decorated edges of the window that displayed the coat of arms of Royalist nobles.

Michaelson bravely condemned the attack from the pulpit soon after, but even then had some sympathy for the aggressors. However, there was little sympathy for him. In 1642, one week before he was thrown into the grave, Parliamentarian soldiers seized the Book of Common Prayer during a service and took it on to the streets, where they did unimaginable things to it. Ironically, they had accidentally picked up the Bible in the first instance and almost ended up desecrating that, only to be stopped by a wiser superior.

Michaelson was threatened again in 1643. Bonfires had been lit in Chelmsford to celebrate the decision in Parliament to abolish episcopacy. The celebrating Parliamentarian soldiers and extremists, the latter under

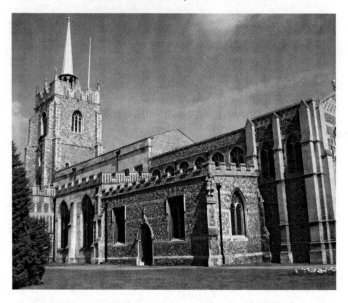

Chelmsford Cathedral.

the influence of alcohol, seized the rector himself on this occasion and headed for the flames. It was clearly their intention to throw him into the fire. Michaelson's friends warned the soldiers' superiors of their intent and the rector was again saved before he could be killed.

However, it proved to be the last straw and Michaelson fled, leaving his family in Chelmsford. His wife and children were held at gunpoint as soldiers searched the rectory for him. The rector first took shelter in Oxford and later moved to Europe. Thanks to his friends, he returned to Chelmsford in 1646, when things had quietened down a bit, taking refuge with his family in a small house at Writtle.

Revd Michaelson did have the last laugh, though he had to wait some time for it. It was not until the Restoration that he was reinstated as rector of St Mary's.

Where There's a Will, There's a Way to Get Your Message Across

Thomas Williamson wanted to make a difference after his death. But surely not even he could have imagined the impact money left in his will was to have on the town of Chelmsford. However, it is probably safe to assume he would have been pleased with what followed in the years following his passing in 1614.

Williamson was a former churchwarden of St Mary's church. He was a well-respected figure in the town, a scholar of the Bible, but from a thesis he published in 1606 against the Church of Rome, he was clearly a man who had his foot in the Protestant camp.

Williamson may not be a name familiar with most Chelmsfordians today. However, if it were not for him – or at least his will – one of the town's most celebrated residents would probably never have set foot here. The name of Thomas Hooker is, unlike that of Williamson, at least familiar to some Chelmsford residents today, if only because they have seen it on a plaque high on a building close to the cathedral.

Hooker came to Chelmsford in 1625 and, though he stayed only a few years, certainly made a name for himself. Of course, it was through his achievements after he left the town that he gained immortal fame, going on to lead a group of pioneers to America where he founded the city of Hartford and the state of Connecticut. Today he is regarded as one of the founding fathers of the United States and American democracy.

It was through the will of Williamson that the Chelmsford lectureship was established. Williamson ordered that a sum of £3 12s from the money he left following his death be used annually to pay for the preaching of monthly sermons in the town, so concerned was he at the rapid decline of morals and godliness. He stipulated that four different ministers, each in turn,

A blue plaque now commemorates the impact Thomas Hooker had on Chelmsford.

should preach three sermons a year. However, by the 1620s, the town appeared to favour a single lecturer to deliver the monthly sermons.

Hooker was a student of Emmanuel College, Cambridge, the Puritan seat of learning established by Chelmsford resident, Sir Walter Mildmay. He already had a reputation as a fine preacher when he was invited to become Chelmsford lecturer in 1625.

The Church was at the time struggling to convince everyone that there was only one building people should be seen in on a Sunday. Drinking was a big problem and many preferred to have a tipple or two than seek spiritual nourishment. Hooker angered the Church of England because of his strong Puritan views, but he also must have caused the High Churchmen much embarrassment in succeeding where they had spectacularly failed. Such was his popularity that people were soon voluntarily vacating the inns in order to hear him speak. He regularly drew large crowds and became a massive hit. Everyone wanted to hear what Hooker had to say, but even though he was filling the pews, not all were happy.

Bishop of London, William Laud, a High Churchman who was determined to enforce conformity to the Book of Common Prayer, was a fierce opponent of Puritanism and became determined to see Hooker off. He succeeded. Hooker was removed from the lectureship by a spiritual court and eventually fled to Holland, before emigrating to America where he was to make an even bigger name for himself.

Chelmsford went in search of a new lecturer, but many turned down the position, presumably because they believed the shoes of Hooker were too big to fill. He was certainly a hard act to follow. It is thought the Chelmsford lectureship finally came to an end in about 1632, but that may have been because the money to pay the preachers had run out, Williamson's annuity possibly having run its course.

However, such was the impact Hooker made in Chelmsford, Thomas Williamson would probably have agreed the money he left to provide the town with a godly and inspirational speaker was money well spent.

The Villager Who Became a National Hero

They are made of strong stuff in Writtle. John Bastwick is evidence of that.

Little remembered today, Bastwick was once proclaimed a national hero, but he had to pay a huge price to win the hearts of the public – notably the loss of his ears!

Bastwick, who was born in Writtle at the end of the sixteenth century, was a devout Puritan. It is said he could have been a literary great, but he turned his pen in the direction of the English bishops, attacking them with venom in a series of tracts. He was of the belief that the Church had abused its power in order to rule over the common man.

It was all a far cry from his early childhood. Bastwick himself remarked that he was brought up to enjoy pursuits normally associated with the Royalists. As a child he danced and took part in swordplay, as well as learning the importance of 'gentlemanly deportment'. As Bastwick said himself: 'I was bred in as great a hatred of Puritans as my tender years were capable of.' However, Bastwick received a Protestant education from a strict Puritan lecturer and his head was turned in that direction forever.

His tracts, printed in Holland in the 1630s, pulled no punches. English bishops were depicted as gluttonous, arrogant and the enemies of God. Bastwick knew it was a dangerous time to write on the subject of religion and that what he wrote would cause outrage. It did.

Bastwick soon found himself before the authorities. He was initially fined £1,000 and sent to prison until he recanted all the charges he had made in his books. Those offending items were burnt. Bastwick, a physician by profession, refused to recant and wrote further tracts while behind bars. One has to admire his courage. He would have known what fate awaited him for further inciting those in power.

Bastwick, along with a couple of other likeminded offenders, was put in the pillory in the yard at the Palace of Westminster and there had both ears cut off. It is said Bastwick, being a medical man, even brought his own scalpel for the task. In front of what was a crowd sympathetic to his plight – people threw flowers into his path on the way to the pillory – Bastwick bowed gracefully before

The peaceful village of Writtle produced a very tough man.

the cruel punishment was carried out. He was then transported to a prison as far away as possible – in his case it was on the Isles of Scilly – where he would be unable to express his radical views to anyone. Even the gaoler was forbidden to speak to him.

Bastwick must have suffered much in his gloomy cell and would have remained there for the rest of his life if the Royalists had won the Civil War. But, in 1640, the Parliamentarians, now in control of the country, reversed his sentence, although they were unable to put his ears back. Bastwick was released from jail and returned to London. Large crowds greeted him, again throwing flowers into his path. To the Parliamentarians, he was a martyr. Bastwick eventually also received financial compensation out of the estates of the Church, which at least meant this brave controversialist and pamphleteer was able to live his final years in relative comfort.

I Will Build My Church … Again … and Again

The collapse of the roof at Chelmsford Cathedral in 1800 – then a mere parish church – is no secret. However, it was not the only church to come tumbling down in that ill-fated year.

Just a few months after the Chelmsford incident, a similar catastrophe occurred at Writtle.

It led locals to come up with the ditty (other versions are available): 'Writtle Tower and Chelmsford Steeple; Both fell down and hurt no people.' Indeed, it was perhaps a miracle no one was hurt in either incident.

St Mary's church, Chelmsford, collapsed on a night in January, which meant that the premises were fortunately unoccupied at the time. The collapse of the roof and nave was blamed on workmen who had been digging a grave too close to supporting pillars earlier in the day.

Writtle church.

In April, it was the turn of All Saints' church in Writtle. People rushed from their homes when they heard a tremendous crash. Part of the tower had collapsed and, later that night, more followed, bringing down the bells with it.

The Gentleman's Magazine was quick to relay the news. In its evening edition on 4 April, a reporter declared: 'This day at noon, the north west corner of the venerable tower of Writtle church in Essex, which had shown for some time past, evident marks of decay, and had been at different times very injudiciously repaired, came down with a most tremendous crash. The humble residents of a cottage near the church very reluctantly quitted their dwelling ten minutes before the fall of the ruin which levelled it to the ground.'

Both churches were restored to their former glory and are to this day still standing strong.

Built to Order

When Jesus Christ commanded his followers to build his church, he did not literally mean with bricks and mortar. However, a Chelmsford housewife did just that, though her place of worship, to be precise, was constructed from wood and corrugated iron.

Throughout the Bible, it is written that God has used 'ordinary' people to carry out his work. Rose Whybrow was no exception. In 1923, she became convinced God was speaking to her. Her testimony records: 'My heart was touched concerning the little children that ran about the roads on the Sabbath day and never had a Sunday school to go to.' Mrs Whybrow believed that God was asking her to start a Sunday school in the village. She started to talk to children as they passed her house and decided to invite them into her home. (One has to remember they were different times back then.) 'Two very shy children' came on the

The chapel built by a determined housewife.

first Sunday. They brought their little brother the following week and then a friend. She told them stories from the Bible and soon her house was not big enough to accommodate all the children. Larger premises were required and Mrs Whybrow still did 'not feel rested'. She was 'feeding' the 'lambs', but felt a voice was telling her to 'feed my sheep' too. She needed premises to accommodate both children and adults, and turned to God for inspiration. Mrs Whybrow set her eyes upon a verse in the Book of Haggai: 'Go up into the mountains and bring down timber and build the house.'

The determined lady came to the conclusion that God wanted her to build a church next to her own home. And, after much bureaucracy was overcome, permission was obtained to do just that at the beginning of 1926.

Bethel Chapel was built at a cost of about £185. It still stands today, in Chignall Road at the junction with the road to Mashbury, although sadly the building is no longer used for services, the Chelmsford Christian Growth Centre that evolved out of it now operating from another venue. In fact, most people are unaware that the humble wooden building was once a church, its green corrugated iron roof a big contrast to the elaborate stone carvings and stained-glass windows that you will find at more traditional places of worship.

Set the World on 'Friar'

You might have expected to find a few secrets within the walls of the Dominican friary that once stood in Moulsham. Men of the habit, in choosing to lead solitary lives, have often been viewed with suspicion and accused of getting up to all sorts of mischief behind their closed doors. The famous monks of the Knights Templar were renowned for their secret and mysterious ways.

And most Chelmsfordians might have expected nothing less from the friars that founded a religious house in Moulsham in the thirteenth century. However, in a bizarre sort of way, the big 'secret' is perhaps that there were probably very few secrets within the walls of the friary that once stood here.

By all accounts, the Black Friars that inhabited these walls were, unlike other orders, far from secretive, and residents of the town appeared to be very fond of them. The friars did not live solitary and contemplative lives, but adopted a policy of openness. Their aim was to provide relief and education for the poor, and they were frequently seen rubbing shoulders with ordinary townsfolk. The brothers certainly did not shut themselves away from the world and welcomed others within their walls as well, including royalty.

Many Chelmsfordians will also be unaware that a very famous theologian and historian once resided here.

A stone memorial is the only visible reminder of the friary that once stood in Moulsham.

Thomas Langford studied at Moulsham as a Dominican friar before moving to Cambridge in about 1320. Langford wrote a history of the world, from Creation to his own times. He also penned a volume of sermons. Langford appears to have taken his name from the village near Maldon where he was born, so little is known about his life, bits and pieces having been put together over the years by chroniclers such as Italian Dominican Leandro Alberti. However, it is clear that Langford became a major religious and literary figure during his day and, though it is not known when he published his universal chronicle, it is quite possible he may have penned at least some of it within the friary walls.

Sadly, nothing remains of Langford's work and nothing visible above ground remains of Moulsham friary either. Along with other great religious houses, it was demolished at the order of Henry VIII during the Dissolution of the Monasteries.

Someone Will Pay For It in the End

Poor Thomas Morgan Gepp was not able to forget the role he had in putting John Thorogood behind bars.

Thorogood became a national celebrity in the mid-nineteenth century for refusing to pay the church rate. Churchwarden Gepp was the man who initiated proceedings against Thorogood, unaware it would lead to the latter becoming a hero – and even a martyr – in the eyes of the public. Thorogood was to spend the good part of two years in prison. People were full of admiration for his stand against the establishment. The church rate he refused to pay was a trifling amount – a mere 5s 6d – but Thorogood refused on principal to pay it. He was adamant that it was wrong for the state to support religion.

Gepp, unable to get the money from Thorogood, felt he was obliged to take action. Thorogood was summoned to appear before an ecclesiastical court. He did not turn up. Deemed to be in contempt of court, Thorogood was imprisoned in Chelmsford. He remained there for about nineteen months. His wife was among those to protest outside the gaol; his case caught the attention of the public and most sided with him. The authorities wanted to end what had become an embarrassment to them, but their hands were tied. The public, without the knowledge of Thorogood, offered to pay the outstanding church rate and raised enough money to cover incurred expenses. However, Thorogood was not actually in prison for not paying the rate, but for contempt of court. Until Thorogood agreed to attend court, he could not be freed. Needless to say, the stubborn and determined Thorogood had no intention of backing down. He wrote from prison: 'I am here, and mean to remain here until death, rather than pay or sanction the payment of one farthing towards that horrid system of priestcraft – an established Church.'

Parliament attempted to resolve the crisis on several occasions. Finally, in the summer of 1840, Thorogood was freed, a special clause required in a bill to allow the case to proceed without Thorogood having to be present. The public eventually paid the 5s 6d and the costs Thorogood had incurred while in prison. The public appeal in aid of Thorogood had raised much money and there was plenty over. On his release, Thorogood was presented with a cheque for £900. He used the money to build a row of stone cottages in Springfield. One supposes Thorogood did not take long to come up with a name for the new properties. On the wall of one of the cottages, in prominent letters, he painted the words 'Gepp's Folly'.

It's Not Always Best to Go First

An opening ceremony should be a celebration. However, when you are 'opening' a cemetery, it is quite a different story. And, of course, there would be very few volunteers to be the first to try it out.

Sadly, and coincidentally, the first person to be laid to rest at the non-conformist cemetery in New London Road was the son of the man who designed it. Poor James Fenton, not long after he had no doubt stood back with pride at his creation, was forced to bury his 11-year-old son James Lionel there following his death on 9 July 1846.

Fenton Sr was a notable architect and engineer, and many of his creations still survive in Chelmsford. He was himself buried in the cemetery he created, following his own death towards the end of the nineteenth century.

My Other Parish Is On the Other Side of the World

It is perhaps safe to assume that a few tongues were set wagging whenever Revd Jack Sparrow, vicar of Highwood, made one of his regular trips to London. Apparently, villagers had no idea what his business in the capital involved.

Incredible as it seems, it is thought most of his parishioners were oblivious to the fact that Revd Sparrow held another post in the 1950s. Not only was he vicar of Highwood – but he was also the deputy bishop of Borneo! Sparrow regularly travelled from Chelmsford to London – to the offices of the BBC World Service, to be precise – in order to broadcast to the people of Borneo in their own tongue. The much-loved clergyman, who spent most of his childhood in Writtle, served in Borneo as a missionary before returning to England and becoming vicar of Highwood, a village just down the road from Writtle.

Revd Sparrow never severed his ties with Borneo and was appointed deputy to the Bishop of Borneo in 1949, a position he held – albeit from a distance – until 1962. His broadcasts from London ensured his 'parishioners' on the other side of the world could still benefit from his words of wisdom.

It is not known why most in Highwood had no idea of his 'second job' or the reason for his 'mysterious' trips to London. It is assumed that Revd Sparrow never spoke of it because of his humility.

Of course, the name Jack Sparrow means little more than a big-screen pirate to most these days, though a few in Writtle and Highwood still fondly remember their Jack Sparrow. A small close in Highwood is named after him, though it is perhaps safe to assume his heart always remained in Borneo and it is fitting that his ashes were sent there following his death in the mid-1960s.

The Revd Jack Sparrow was not only vicar of St Paul's church, Highwood.

A 'Knight' To Remember

The memory of the remarkable Anne Knight lives on in Chelmsford. However, few know that it also lives on across the Atlantic ... in Jamaica.

Most Chelmsford residents will have at least heard of the name Anne Knight and commuters rushing to the railway station would have passed the Quaker Meeting House, where she worshipped many times. The building is now named after her. Of course, not so many people know exactly what she did or why her name lives on in a place so removed from Chelmsford.

Anne Knight was a campaigner who devoted her life to not one, but two worthy causes. A slavery abolitionist, she also turned to fighting for the rights of women, long before the likes of Emmeline Pankhurst.

Anne was born to a family of Quakers and spent her early life in Springfield. She became deeply involved in the anti-slavery movement, travelling to London and Europe to speak against the slave trade. She soon gained a reputation as a leading slavery abolitionist, but there was one major hindrance to her battle – she was a woman.

Anne lived in what was still a man's world and this very fact was emphasised at the World Anti-Slavery Convention in London in 1840. Though Anne was able to meet and mix with prominent American abolitionists there, she and the other female delegates were prevented from taking part in the discussion itself. Instead, she had to listen to the views of her male counterparts and remain silent.

It was to be a defining moment for both Anne and the emancipation of women. Some historians date the movement for women's suffrage in Britain from that anti-slavery convention. That high-profile abolitionists like Anne were prevented from sharing their much respected views drew attention to the marginal status of women in society. It highlighted the limitations imposed on a woman working in the public domain. Their hands remained tied. The first women's rights convention in the United States was soon held, in New York in 1848.

Some believe Anne to be the author of a famous anonymous letter printed in Britain the previous year in which the writer announced: 'Never will the nations of the earth be well governed, until both sexes, as well as all parties, are fully represented and have an influence, a voice, and a hand in the enactment and administration of the laws.'

Anne was, not surprisingly, involved in the forming of the first organisation for women's suffrage in Britain – the Sheffield Female Political Association – that was set up in 1851. By this time Anne had in fact left Chelmsford for France, where she continued to campaign for the rights of both slaves and women. She returned to Chelmsford on occasions to give speeches and remained devoted to both causes until her death in 1862.

The life work of Anne Knight did bear fruit, of course. Today women have a lot to thank her for. And, in Jamaica, she lives on. A village that was founded for freed slaves was named Knightsville in honour of this very determined former Chelmsfordian.

Cast One's Vote ... Into the River

Election time fills many with dread these days. Few would use the word 'fun' to describe it. However, Chelmsford once knew how to have a good time whenever there was a general election.

The town held its own mock election at the same time. It was known as the Mesopotamia Election due to its venue. Mesopotamia Island once sat on what is now land east of the high street between the River Chelmer and River Can. The island is no secret, but many today have no idea it once existed, and those that do have often, no doubt, wondered how it got its name. The answer is very simple: Mesopotamia means 'land between rivers'.

Two candidates were selected and hustings erected outside the Duke's Head Inn to enable them to make their speeches, usually with tongue firmly in cheek. The candidates were dubbed knights and given noble names to suit their real occupations. For example, a fishmonger might be called Sir Thomas Trout or a greengrocer Sir Charles Cabbage. The 'knights' were paraded on horseback throughout the town, each attended by their own page. Followers of the candidates encouraged the public to vote for their man, and voters were charged a penny for the privilege of casting their vote.

At the end of the day the result was announced. The successful candidate would be chaired through the town on the shoulders of their followers. The unsuccessful candidate would usually be ducked in the river. It appears the winner also suffered this same fate, but was at least allowed to keep the pennies for his efforts.

It might be an idea to revive the custom, but instead replace the mock candidates with the real ones. Certainly, more people might be inclined to take an interest if they knew the politicians would receive a ducking at the end of it!

War

The Local 'Takeaway'

The Siege of Colchester in 1648 was one of the most dramatic events of the Civil War. For some three months, the Royalists and many innocent residents were imprisoned within the town walls, surrounded by the Parliamentarian army of General Sir Thomas Fairfax. Once the food had gone, they were forced to eat cats and dogs – and even rats – before the Royalists eventually surrendered, Fairfax succeeding in his plan to 'starve them out'.

The event is no secret and you perhaps could be forgiven for questioning what it had to do with the town of Chelmsford. However, what is not widely known is that within those town walls of Colchester were a number of Chelmsford hostages.

Essex did not see a lot of action during the First Civil War. However, when Charles I escaped from Hampton Court and fled to the Isle of Wight, his followers gained renewed optimism. It was to lead to the Second Civil War.

The Royalists soon assembled a huge army at Chelmsford and, in the summer of 1648, Parliament was informed that a standing committee in the town had been taken by surprise during one of its sessions. The Royalists seized the committee members by violence and forced them to send a written message ordering the Parliamentarian army not to advance against the king's men.

With their hostages, the Royalists left Chelmsford and headed east. Fairfax did not submit to their order and followed them, eventually surrounding the king's men within the town walls of Colchester. He knew they would have to come out sooner or later. The Royalists must have also known that their days were numbered. They had to resort to sorties after dark to replenish supplies, but soon Fairfax succeeded in cutting off every possible route open to them. It was not just the Royalists who suffered. Many residents were trapped with them, not to mention the Chelmsford hostages.

The surrender only came after eleven weeks, during which many people are said to have starved to death.

Parliament was informed in early July that the Chelmsford committee members were 'in sore straits'. They were not released until the end of August under the terms of the final Royalist surrender and so one can only imagine what condition they must have been in by then.

A 'Common' Cause

Galleywood Common is all about peace and quiet these days. It is an ideal place to forget your troubles and, though just a short walk from the city centre, seemingly a world away. It was not like that some 200 years ago, however.

Many who take a stroll on the common today do so without the faintest idea of what once stood here. That is perhaps no surprise. The only trace of the huge artillery fort that graced this spot is the remains of earthworks, now mostly hidden among trees. The average resident would be quite surprised to learn Chelmsford was once very fearful of an enemy invasion by sea. After all, the city sits slap-bang in the middle of the county and a long way from the coast.

However, prior to and during the Napoleonic Wars, the French would have viewed the town as a prime target. Should the forces of Napoleon have got past the British navy and landed on our shores, many believed they would have headed for Chelmsford. It was thought the enemy would have needed a base close to London in order to prepare for the big attack on the capital. Chelmsford, some 30 miles away, would have been a perfect spot.

Two barracks for soldiers were built at the end of the eighteenth century on what are now Wood Street and Roxwell Road. Both could hold about 4,000 men. An unbroken barrier – of more than 2 miles – was set up just beyond Wood Street in Widford and arced towards

Galleywood Common. Two massive forts were built at each end of 'The Lines', the name given to the defences. The Galleywood fort was larger than its Widford counterpart and could hold almost 1,000 men.

The threat of an attack was very real; people lived in fear of an impending invasion. By 1803, Napoleon had amassed a huge army at Boulogne on the northern French coast. Boats were ready to take his troops across the Channel.

Of course, the invasion never materialised. Most will know of Lord Nelson's famous victory at the Battle of Trafalgar in 1805 and, with most of the French fleet destroyed, Britain no longer needed to fear an imminent attack from the Continent. Ironically, the threat

The Galleywood fort earthworks.

of an attack diminished almost immediately after the Chelmsford defences were completed: French military strategy had changed even before Nelson's triumph. Protecting Chelmsford did not come cheap, but residents believed it had been a price worth paying. Locals apparently raised a massive £10,000 to help build up the town's defences.

The Galleywood fort was situated on relatively high ground. Galleywood Windmill was left standing within its walls, as it proved to be a useful lookout post. Soldiers stationed in the area carried out building work themselves. The fort consisted of earth banks up to 20ft wide in places. The inner face of the ditch was lined with sharp wooden stakes that were laid horizontally. It would have been some fortress.

With the threat of Napoleon gone, the Chelmsford forts became redundant and it was not long before they were demolished. Apart from the earthworks, there is now little evidence of the fort that once stood at Galleywood. However, it appears Watchouse Road gained its name from what once went on at this now peaceful part of Chelmsford.

War and No Peace

It was not so much the French that Chelmsfordians lived in fear of at the beginning of the nineteenth century. Many residents were more fearful of the very men that had been hired to protect them.

The Treaty of Amiens in 1802 brought a temporary halt to the war with France. It left thousands of soldiers garrisoned at Chelmsford kicking their heels. They had seen no action and, with time on their hands, discipline among troops became lapse, many turning to drink to while away the hours. That in turn led to drunkenness and unsocial behaviour.

There were numerous reports of soldiers turning on the citizens they were supposed to be protecting. It was not just loutish behaviour. Soldiers sporting bayonets robbed residents in the narrow and dark lanes near their barracks.

A special court was held to get to the root of the problem. Victims and witnesses gave evidence to the magistrates, but little changed. The garrison officers were told to improve discipline, but the problem continued. The terrified locals decided to go to a higher authority with their complaint, to none less than Prince Frederick, Duke of York and Albany, commander-in-chief of the forces. The duke – in charge of the British army when it had a poor reputation – is now fondly remembered as the 'grand old Duke of York' in the nursery rhyme. He ordered an investigation and employed Major-General John Moore – who later died a hero at the Battle of Corunna in 1809 – to carry it out. Moore knew the town well, having himself been stationed at Chelmsford a few years earlier. He produced a damning report on the regiment he had been asked to investigate. However, it was not so much the soldiers who received the blame, but their commanding officers. As well as setting an appalling example of ill-discipline, the officers were also accused of covering up the crimes of the offending soldiers.

The report was presented to King George III himself and, in a bid to end the scandal, the commander of the under-fire regiment was forced to apologise in public. The regiment was withdrawn from Chelmsford and the barracks remained empty until the war with France resumed.

Dig Deep for Victory

It seems the people of Chelmsford have always been a generous lot. They certainly 'dug deep' during

Warship Week in February 1942. As part of the war effort, councils throughout Britain were asked to adopt a vessel. Chelmsford set its sights on not one, but two.

It was a tall order. A target of £240,000 was set. Residents had just seven days to come up with the cash. However, in the end, a massive £770,710 was raised. Chelmsford had intended to adopt two corvettes – HMS *Cyclamen* and HMS *Coriander*. However, there was much disappointment when the Admiralty informed the council that it would not allow one area to adopt two vessels. The mayor of Chelmsford was not amused. He wrote to the Admiralty to protest.

It worked. Chelmsford received the news that it would get a second vessel, one more appropriate to the excellent fundraising efforts of the residents, a destroyer called HMS *Hardy*. And so the borough council adopted *Hardy* and the rural district council adopted *Cyclamen*.

While *Cyclamen* survived the war, *Hardy* was not so fortunate. The torpedo of a U-boat in the Barents Sea hit her at the beginning of 1944 and she was sunk by a coup de grâce.

Bombs Won't Stop Play

Chelmsford was targeted by the Germans during the Second World War. Many lost their lives as the bombs fell. However, life went on. And where better would you find a British 'stiff upper lip' than at a golf club, a very British institution.

There was no way that members of Chelmsford Golf Club, like many up and down the country, were going to let the enemy prevent them from enjoying a round. However, the club at Widford, like others, was forced to amend some of its rules. One rule at the time read: 'A player whose stroke is affected by the simultaneous explosion of a bomb or shell, or by machine-gun fire, may play another ball from the same place.'

A Good Time to Come Home

The outbreak of the First World War might have been a blessing in disguise for a former owner of Hylands House. The War Office requisitioned the grand property to use as a temporary hospital, prompting Sir Daniel Fulthorpe Gooch to cut short his travels abroad in order to oversee the conversion of his home. It was probably a wise move.

The adventurous Gooch was at the time a member of the crew of the *Endurance*, the ship that came unstuck (or should I say stuck) under the command of Ernest Shackleton. Gooch, the grandson of a famous railway engineer who shared the same name, was a last-minute replacement for the doomed Imperial Trans-Antarctic Expedition. The man selected to look after the sixty-nine dogs needed for the voyage withdrew at the eleventh hour and Shackleton turned to Gooch, an old friend, to replace him. Gooch was a keen sportsman, a follower of the hunt, and an expert in breeding dogs, but he had no polar experience. He signed up as an able seaman and surely there have been few knights of the realm at sea bearing that lowly rank. He originally set sail from Liverpool, with the dogs, joining up with the *Endurance* in Buenos Aires.

However, Gooch left the expedition in South Georgia to return to Chelmsford. Shackleton wrote: 'We all regretted losing his cheery presence when we sailed for the South.' Of course, disaster was to hit the expedition. The *Endurance* became stuck in the ice and eventually sank. Though there was no loss of life, the crew endured a torrid time. They did not set foot on solid ground for 497 days.

Hylands – now a place for recreation – has had many uses over the years.

As an emergency hospital, Hylands House was able to accommodate almost 200 beds. About 1,500 wounded soldiers were treated there before the war came to an end.

Who Dares 'Loses'

The motto of the SAS (Special Air Service) – 'who dares wins' – has no doubt been an inspiration to many members. However, on at least one occasion, one member of that renowned organisation who dared certainly did not end up winning.

Hylands House became the secret headquarters of the SAS during the Second World War, having been formed in 1941. One of the founder members was

Paddy Mayne, who went on to become one of Britain's most highly decorated soldiers, but was controversially denied a Victoria Cross. Mayne was commander when the SAS came to Hylands House in 1944.

Christine Hanbury owned the property at the time. She threw herself into the war effort after her son Jock, an RAF pilot, was killed just a few weeks into the hostilities. His widow Felicity Hanbury (later Peake) went on to become the founding director of the Women's Royal Air Force.

It is said that Mrs Hanbury was happy to accommodate the newly formed SAS, with Mayne and his troops occupying the ground floor and cellars while she continued to reside on the upper floor. She got on well with the regiment and was often invited to dine with the officers.

While the SAS has always been regarded as a very serious organisation, its members apparently also knew how to party, Mayne being no exception. He had a reputation for hard drinking and was not someone to be messed with after a drink or two. There are endless stories of him taking on – and beating – anyone who dared step outside with him after a night at the bar.

One night, no doubt after a little too much to drink, Mayne accepted a bet to drive a jeep up the main staircase at Hylands House. Presumably, the SAS motto was ringing in his ears and he dared not turn down the dare. However, Mayne spectacularly failed to win the bet, the jeep becoming wedged in a right turn on the staircase. Needless to say, Mrs Hanbury was not amused. She ordered the men to bed. In the morning, with clearer heads, Mayne and his troops attempted to dislodge the offending jeep, but it proved a fruitless task and it could only be removed by dismantling it.

Mrs Hanbury was the last private owner of Hylands House. She remained there until her death in 1962.

Chelmsford Borough Council bought the estate a few years later and opened it to the public.

A Shot In The Dark

It is perhaps odd that Chelmsford should proudly display a cannon from the Crimean War in Oaklands Park.

However, it is no secret, and the Sebastopol Cannon has become one of the town's most familiar sights, it once being situated in a far more prominent position outside the Shire Hall.

What perhaps sets it apart from other 'captured' remnants of war on display throughout the country is the fact that the mouth of this particular cannon is now blocked up. There is perhaps a good reason for this. Sightseers will not doubt that the cannon was fired many times in the heat of the battle at Sebastopol, but they might not know it was also fired in Chelmsford.

The Sebastopol Cannon in Oaklands Park.

Some high-spirited youngsters decided to test it out one evening in 1908 when it was situated outside the Shire Hall. The youths primed the cannon with gunpowder and fired it. Fortunately, the practical joke did not cause any injury, but there were reports of many damaged windows and the collapse of a ceiling in a shop close by.

The mouth of the cannon was subsequently sealed and it was eventually relocated to its current position. However, sealed it may now be, it might not have been the wisest move to have positioned it pointing directly at the city museum, one of Chelmsford's top attractions!

Travel and Transport

The Other Way

Few who tread an often-muddy bridle path in Writtle have any idea of the major role it has played in the history of Chelmsford. It is merely the haunt of the occasional horse rider or dog walker today. Few use it as a short cut; a surfaced cycleway and footpath from St John's Road connects the village to the city centre these days. However, it was not always like that.

Lollefordstrat – now known simply as Lawford Lane – was responsible for almost making the village of Writtle, and not Chelmsford itself, the county town of Essex. It was not until around 1100 that Maurice, the Bishop of London, famously built a bridge over the River Can in what is now the city centre that Chelmsford began to prosper at the expense of Writtle. Until then, Writtle was the more important place, due to the fact that the Colchester to London Roman road went through Writtle, via Lollefordstrat.

The new bridge cannot be solely blamed for the decline of Writtle in terms of importance, but it meant it was no longer necessary for travellers to take a detour around the Can. The bridge significantly shortened the route to London, and Chelmsford grew as the principal settlement between the capital and the East of England.

The ford at Writtle that the early travellers crossed now has a bridge itself in order to stop people getting their feet wet. And it is particularly required after heavy rain, as the area is still prone to flooding.

That we know Maurice was presumably responsible for building a bridge over the Can is in part thanks to a former Chelmsfordian. Philemon Holland was responsible for the English translation, from Latin, of William Camden's *Britannia*, the work informing us that Maurice's bridge 'turned the London way thither'.

Looking at the Lawford Lane bridle path today it is difficult to believe it was once the 'king's highway to London'. However, it was not until well into the second half of the nineteenth century that it officially lost its status as a 'high road'.

The 'Incline' and Fall of the Roman Empire

Many visitors – and even some residents – are not aware that Chelmsford was once a Roman town. Unlike nearby Colchester, with its famous Roman walls, there are no obvious remains above ground. Of course, you will find plenty of evidence at the local museum of what lay underground and clues to what may still lie there. Excavations of archaeologists in recent years have unearthed many treasures.

However, to say there is no visible reminder above ground of Roman Chelmsford is not strictly true. You just have to know where to look. The street name 'Roman Road' is a big help, but take a walk down this particular thoroughfare in Moulsham and you will probably still be oblivious to the fact that the remains of a very important

There is now a bridge over the ford which early travellers were forced to cross.

Roman building lie beneath. The only visible evidence of the once grand *mansio* that stood here is a slight incline in the road itself. The slope of the platform on which the *mansio* was built, created by terracing the ground, is not difficult to spot if you are looking for it.

The *mansio* dominated the Roman settlement here. A *mansio* was an official stopping-place on a Roman road, in this case the road between London and Colchester. Travellers on business would have been able to have a bath and a bed for the night. Excavations have established it was once a very grand building, with rooms situated around a central courtyard. With such an important building and the fact the Roman settlement here was named Caesaromagus, it is something of a mystery why the town never grew to become very large.

It must have been a place of importance to the Romans. It was, after all, the only place in Britain to bear the name of the famous emperor. Sitting conveniently between London and Colchester, the capital of Roman Britain at the time, it seemed to have everything going for it. The *mansio* was built with stone, again emphasising its importance, as stone was rare in Essex and only used for the most important buildings.

Some have suggested Caesaromagus was a Roman 'new town' that failed, which may explain why it apparently remained merely a stopping place and never really developed in its own right.

When the Romans left Britain, it is believed Caesaromagus was abandoned, the Saxons preferring to settle in the surrounding countryside. It was not until Norman times that Chelmsford started to prosper and begin to develop into the city we now know.

You can still trace evidence of the Romans in Roman Road.

Bridge of Size

It took more than 400 years for the bridge connecting Chelmsford with Moulsham to be widened. Not until the 1372 bridge of Henry Yevele was replaced in the 1780s by John Johnson's stone bridge – now one of the most familiar landmarks in the city – did the road over the River Can gain those much-needed extra inches.

Even when Yevele built his structure in the fourteenth century, most recognised the fact that the original ancient bridge it was to replace was too narrow. It was therefore widened. However, an innkeeper called Thomas Ostler claimed it had been done so at the expense of his adjoining property and so later 'took back' the extra inches. A dispute raged for many years and was only settled in court, the Ostler family finally winning the day, with the result that the bridge remained too narrow to cope with increasing amounts of traffic.

However, some four centuries later, the authorities should have been grateful for the stubborn resistance of the Ostler family as the narrowness of the bridge helped to catch a suspected member of the notorious Gregory Gang. The gang terrorised Essex and one of its former members was none less than the infamous Dick Turpin himself. One day in 1735, at least two members of the gang were fleeing capture on horseback. The men were chased towards the bridge of Yevele. The first managed to get ahead of a wagon heading for the bridge and overtook it just in time to make his escape. However, his accomplice was not so lucky. He reached the bridge at the same time as the wagon and attempted to squeeze past, but, due to the narrowness of the bridge, was unable to do so, with the result that his horse became wedged in between the wagon and a post. The fugitive was unable to free his steed, which gave his pursuers the time they needed to catch up with him.

The new bridge was built using 250 tonnes of Portland stone, shipped from Dorset to Maldon and then carried by cart to Chelmsford. Among those to help build it was a woman, something that would have been unusual in those days. Sarah Wray was the widow of prominent stonemason George Wray. Following his death, she took over the business until their son, also called George, was old enough to take control, as was customary at the time.

In order to widen the bridge, part of a house on the site of the building once occupied by the Ostlers had to be pulled down. Fortunately, the owners agreed to sell on this occasion. The new stone bridge was wide enough to also accommodate footways on either side. However, it is perhaps ironic that its extra width

There is plenty of room on Stone Bridge these days.

is not really needed today, since traffic along the road is prohibited following the pedestrianisation of the town centre.

From a Distance

John Rennie is known among Chelmsfordians as the man responsible for the Chelmer and Blackwater Navigation. However, the modest Rennie – the chief canal engineer of the day – insisted he had little to do with it.

As the engineer hired to design the navigation that was to connect the county town of Essex with the tidal estuary of the River Blackwater, you might be forgiven for thinking that Rennie was a regular visitor to Chelmsford at the end of the eighteenth century. However, even though the project took four years to complete, you could have counted on one hand the amount of times he came to cast his eye on the scheme. Rennie did everything from a distance.

Chelmsford residents might also not be aware of the fact that it actually took some 120 years to build the navigation. There was talk of a scheme to link Chelmsford with the sea as early as 1677. Plans for a navigable waterway from Maldon to Chelmsford were produced on numerous occasions over the years, but nothing came of them, with Maldon residents being particularly opposed. Chelmsford relied on goods being transported by road from Maldon, and those responsible for these tasks feared losing their jobs.

However, in 1792, the idea was brought up again and Rennie agreed to take on the job, but only from a distance. He said he was too busy working on other canal projects to devote too much time to it. Rennie did not even conduct the initial survey. He hired surveyor Charles Wedge for that purpose and compiled his own report from Wedge's findings.

Rennie, in his report, recommended straightening, widening and deepening the existing channel of the river, rather than cutting an independent canal. He then recommended another engineer to take charge locally and, because there were no emails or mobile phones in those days, kept in touch by post. However, his letters were meticulously written, his instructions containing every little detail. He wrote from all over the country, but is thought to have only visited the project a few times himself. Rennie was in control from start to finish, and always had the final say, but he himself declared that he could scarcely claim to have had a hand in it.

The Chelmer and Blackwater Navigation, some 14 miles long, finally opened in 1797. It was a huge success. Industries sprang up at Springfield Basin, its Chelmsford terminus, such as iron foundries, sawmills, coal merchants and gasworks.

It is perhaps ironic that the canal played a part in its own demise. When the railway came to Chelmsford in the 1840s, the canal was at its busiest, transporting materials for the building work. However, when the railway became operational, businesses soon discovered that the train was a much quicker way of transporting goods and canal traffic steadily declined. Like most canals throughout Britain, the Chelmer and Blackwater Navigation is now home to pleasure boats these days and makes for fine nature walks. Sightseers can still marvel at the handiwork of John Rennie, even if, it appears, he was too busy to marvel at it himself.

Train of Thought

Those in charge of Chelmsford during the mid-nineteenth century cannot be accused of being short-sighted. Many in Britain viewed the arrival of the railway with suspicion.

And many towns and cities are still, even today, paying a price because their forefathers did not put their faith in it.

The fact that Chelmsford station today sits in the city centre is testament to the town's forward-thinking councillors. The town of Chelmsford was different from others. It embraced the railway wholeheartedly. Clearly, the authorities saw it as the future and allowed

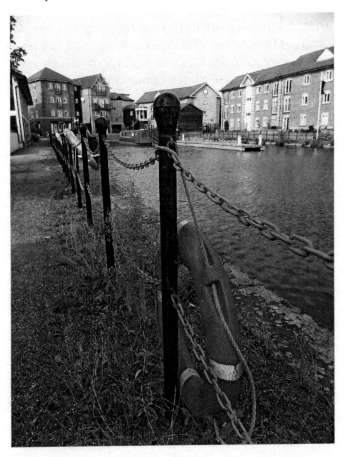

Springfield Basin – the Chelmsford terminus of the Chelmer and Blackwater Navigation.

the station to be built in the centre of the town, though the original one was in a different position to the one in use today. At the time – the railway came to Chelmsford in 1843 – most towns and cities opted to build their stations on the outskirts. Rather than it playing an important role in the life of the people, it was viewed to be almost an intrusion or interference.

Visitors to Chelmsford today will step off the platform and find themselves in Duke Street, right in the city centre. Many towns and cities in Britain do not have that luxury and still rue the actions of their ancestors in refusing to allow the railway to go right through their town.

Chelmsford went to great lengths to ensure trains would be able to stop in the centre of the town, constructing huge viaducts that still carry passengers above the rooftops. It is said that more than 10 million bricks were used to build them.

Trains still enter the city above the rooftops.

The Next Stop Is My House

If your train had been a few minutes late in the nine-teenth century, you might have been able to blame Sir John Tyrell of Boreham House. There is a chance he might have stopped it as it passed through his estate. You would not have been able to complain, though, for it was well within his rights to do just that.

In 1838, the canny Tyrell struck a deal with the Eastern Counties Railway (ECR). In recompense for the new railway passing through his estate, and the damage that would cause, he negotiated certain privileges for himself. One of them was for the ECR to build him a private station on his estate. In truth, it was a mere shed, rather than a station, but it meant he was able to catch a train without leaving his property. He insisted on having the right to stop and board or alight a train at any time when it passed his station. The ECR agreed to his terms and the privilege lasted until his death in 1877, though it is not known how often Tyrell exercised his right to 'hail' a train in those forty years or so. The station was demolished almost immediately after his funeral.

The Man Who Missed the Bus

The name of Thomas Clarkson might have been known throughout the world today if he had come up with his invention a little sooner. It is now no longer even recog-nised in Chelmsford by most.

Clarkson was a pioneer of modern bus travel. After moving to the town in 1902, he produced a prototype steam omnibus that he called *Chelmsford*. At first there was little interest until a group of Torquay businessmen, after viewing one of his demonstrations, asked Clarkson to alter the design to accommodate more passengers, his original only having room for eight. Clarkson drew up a new model to take more people and it was not long before it was driven out of his factory all the way to Devon for a trial run. The trial was successful and Clarkson was asked to build more.

Buses bearing the name *Chelmsford* were to go all over the world in the following years, including India and New Zealand. He even produced double-deckers for the capital. However, perhaps ironically, Clarkson's vehicles were still not carrying passengers in Chelmsford. It was not until 1913, some eight years or more after he had supplied steam buses for routes in Devon, that his home town was to benefit from his expertise.

At its peak, there were 184 Clarkson steam buses operating throughout Britain. However, Clarkson had perhaps himself just missed the bus. Steam had had its day and, by 1920, petrol engines had all but replaced it. Clarkson had come up with a brilliant invention – just a little bit too late.

Fly Me to the (Honey)Moon

In the summer of 1912, a newlywed couple emerged from Widford church on the edge of Hylands Park. The bride and groom were showered with confetti.

You might think there is nothing unusual or strange about that. However, this was no ordinary wedding and that aforementioned confetti had, in fact, been dropped from the sky by an aeroplane.

Claude Grahame-White, the bridegroom, was the most celebrated aviator of the time and it was perhaps only fitting he should have Britain's first 'aero wedding', as the press dubbed it. It has to be remembered flying was in its infancy – few people had even seen an aeroplane – and Chelmsford residents must have watched in awe. Many of the guests, fellow airmen, arrived via aeroplanes, landing on the lawns of Hylands House,

Wedding guests arrived at Widford church, but not by car, one special day in 1912.

the venue of the lavish reception. Grahame-White himself arrived by air.

All the top aviators of the day packed St Mary's church and, following the reception, jumped into their aeroplanes to provide locals with an impromptu air show. The wedding made the front pages of newspapers, both at home and abroad, such was the fame of the bridegroom. Grahame-White fitted the role of aviation hero very well. His good looks and natural charm made him a hit with the ladies. He was huge in the United States and it was rumoured that American ladies were willing to pay up to $500 to be a passenger in his plane.

In England, Grahame-White developed the London Aerodrome at Hendon, which effectively became the home of British aviation. Displays and races became regular events there.

The lucky lady to finally win the heart of the debonair Grahame-White was Dorothy Taylor, a New York socialite. Sadly, the marriage ended in divorce after just a few years.

St Mary's church today stands on the edge of the Hylands estate, pinned in by two busy roads taking cars in and out of the city centre. Those that attempt to get to the church these days, particularly if they are sitting in traffic, might think Grahame-White and his guests had the right idea in choosing to arrive by air.

Strictly Come Dancing

There are many ways to get to Chelmsford. Visitors drive, cycle, catch the train or bus, or merely walk in. However, few arrive as charmingly as William Kemp did in 1599. Kemp danced into town – all the way from Norwich.

William Kemp was an actor by trade. He was one of the original players in the early dramas of no less than William Shakespeare. He excelled at comic roles and was also renowned for his stage jigs. To say he was an eccentric character would probably be an understatement.

Towards the end of his life, Kemp took it upon himself to morris dance all the way from Norwich to London, a distance of more than 100 miles. Chelmsford was upon the route he set himself. It took Kemp nine days of dancing to complete his unusual challenge. However, those nine days were spread over a number of weeks. He arrived in Chelmsford on a Friday and ended up staying for the weekend. It appears the residents did not want him to leave. Kemp described his journey to the capital in *Nine Days Wonder*, which he published in 1600. On arriving at Widford Bridge, he wrote that the people were out in force to greet him, including Sir Thomas Mildmay, the lord of the manor, who took possession of some Kemp 'souvenirs': a pair of garters. Kemp carried merchandise to 'put out to vender for performance of my merry voyage'.

Such was the excitement of the people in Chelmsford that the dancing Kemp was prevented from reaching his inn for more than an hour. He then had to lock the door of his room 'and pacify them with words out of a window instead of deeds: to deal plainly, I was so weary, that I could dance no more'.

Kemp set off towards Braintree the following morning, but had only gone 3 miles when he headed back to Chelmsford, no doubt much to the delight of his many adoring fans. Still exhausted from his exertions, he decided to stay the weekend. 'The good cheer and kind welcome I had at Chelmsford was much more than I was willing to entertain, for my only desire was to refrain drink and be temperate in my diet,' he wrote.

Kemp did give at least one more performance, permitting a young girl, not even 14, to dance with him in a large room. He revealed that the young maid lasted for about an hour before she was too tired to continue. 'I would have challenged the strongest man in Chelmsford, and amongst many I think few would have done so much,' he insisted.

Kemp finally left Chelmsford on the Monday morning. It was only a brief visit, but few who have come to town over the years can have made such an impression. It is safe to say the fun-loving William Kemp had the people of Chelmsford literally dancing in the streets!

Sport and Entertainment

That's the Way the Ball Bounces

In 1991, a basketball was dribbled all the way from Belfast to Chelmsford to celebrate the centenary of the sport. The Church of All Saints at Springfield Green seems, on the surface, an odd place to have ended the British leg of the novel tour. However, it was, in fact, the perfect location.

Puritan William Pynchon was a warden at the church in the first half of the seventeenth century. And he can claim to have played a small part in the invention of the sport in 1891.

Indeed, it was in Springfield that Dr James Naismith invented basketball. Not Springfield, Chelmsford, but Springfield, Massachusetts.

Pynchon was born at Springfield, the Essex one, in 1590. He was the son of a wealthy family that owned land in a number of Chelmsford villages, including Springfield, Broomfield, Writtle and Widford. In 1630, Pynchon and his family sailed across the Atlantic to New England in search of a better life. He became a leading citizen of a new plantation near Boston called Roxbury. However, in the mid-1630s, Pynchon led a group of residents from Roxbury and other communities to a new site. Its location helped Pynchon to make a fortune. Being the most westerly settlement in Massachusetts Bay, there was less interference from the Bay authorities. He had far more power than those in charge of plantations closer to Boston. As the northernmost settlement on the Connecticut River, Pynchon – already a successful fur trader – gained almost complete control of a huge area of New England. The former churchwarden of Springfield, Essex, became very powerful, both in economic and political terms. He was effectively the man in charge, his many roles including that of magistrate.

Pynchon became too powerful for some. His strong religious views were printed in a book in 1650, which the Bay authorities deemed to be heretical. The book was burnt and became the first book of the New World to be banned. That was perhaps the moment that persuaded Pynchon to move back to England for good. He returned to British shores soon after, but did not return to Springfield, Chelmsford. He died in 1662, but not before penning a number of controversial religious pamphlets.

Pynchon had certainly left his mark across the Atlantic. Springfield grew into a town and is now a thriving city. It has many claims to fame. The Springfield-based Smith & Wesson arms factory has produced many weapons. The Springfield rifle also originated there, along with the gas-powered car. The city quickly became famous for the development of transport. And, of course, it was in Springfield, Massachusetts, that Dr Naismith started bouncing a ball and hit upon an idea for a game that now has universal appeal.

Village Was Once in Pole Position

Thousands flock to Silverstone for the British Grand Prix every year. Chelmsford residents may not realise it, but Formula 1 fans might have been coming to their city if things had been just a little bit different. The West Essex Car Club applied to stage the 1953 British Grand Prix at Boreham, on the outskirts of Chelmsford. The future of the circuit at Silverstone was, at the time, not assured. Many were already tipping Boreham, which had been successfully staging motor racing for a few years, as a possible replacement. Sadly, Boreham had had its day by the end of 1952 and, not only did it fail in its bid to stage the British Grand Prix in the following year, but all racing there suddenly came to an abrupt end.

Airfields throughout the country became redundant following the end of the Second World War. They made ideal circuits for motor racing, with airfields at Silverstone and Boreham put to that use. The former US airfield at Boreham became one of the country's premier racing circuits for both motorcars and motorcycles. Thousands flocked to meetings between 1950 and 1952 and it became a serious rival to the already established Silverstone circuit in Northamptonshire. The world's top drivers of the time – Stirling Moss, Roy Salvadori and Ken Wharton – were among those to compete in Essex.

However, it was a young Mike Hawthorn who starred in the biggest event ever staged at Boreham to well and truly announce he had arrived on the world stage. The Daily Mail International Festival of Motor Sport in the summer of 1952 was expected to attract 100,000 motor sport fans to the outskirts of Chelmsford. That figure was not achieved – and the exact number of spectators is still disputed – but certainly more than 50,000 were in attendance. It was still a quality event and *Autocar* reported that 'such a day's motor sport is very rare in Britain'. The press dubbed the event the 'Clash of the Stars'.

The peaceful village of Boreham almost became home to the British Grand Prix.

The upcoming Hawthorn and Moss did battle in the race for Formula 1 and Formula 2 cars. Hawthorn won the latter class, with Moss having to settle for third place. A couple of weeks later, during the Dutch Grand Prix, Hawthorn discovered motor racing giants Ferrari were interested in his services. And, some six years later, Hawthorn, driving for Ferrari, was to become Britain's first Formula 1 world champion.

Of course, motor racing in the early 1950s was very different to modern motor racing. Health and safety officers of today would have been horrified. At Boreham during the International Festival of Motor Sport event, one of the cars – driven by Ian Stewart – slid off the track and through inadequate crash barriers (bundles of hay) into the crowd. It was incredible that nobody was killed. It was reported that seven people were injured, four having sustained broken legs. Perhaps even more incredible was the fact that the race was not stopped and the injured were treated as the cars continued to whiz by.

Silverstone had grown thanks to the backing of the *Daily Express* and, when its rival, the *Daily Mail*, decided to back Boreham, the latter appeared to have the world of motor racing at its feet. However, for a variety of reasons – mostly of a financial nature – motor sport at Boreham came to an end before 1952 had come to an end. A couple of motorcycle meetings took place following the International Festival of Motor Sport, but the likes of Hawthorn and Moss were never again to compete there.

The Ford Motor Company took over the circuit after racing ended. As for Silverstone, it went on to even greater things, though it is not unrealistic to say that if things had worked out differently, the home of British motor racing could have been at Chelmsford.

The Sporting Life

The gravestone of Robert Cook offers more than a few clues as to what field – or should we say fields – his talents could be found in. To say Cook was an all-round sportsman is almost an understatement. He was not only a jack-of-all-trades – but a master of all as well. The tombstone of Cook, which can be found in Chelmsford cemetery, is adorned with carvings of various tools of his trades, from a cricket bat to golf clubs.

Cook was known as the 'Kaiser of Essex sport'. He dominated the county sporting scene in the late nineteenth century. He excelled at every sport he took part in – winning many trophies – but also did much to develop sport in general, both as an administrator and organiser. It has to be remembered that sport in those days was not looked upon in the same light as it is today, and many of his time even wondered whether it had any use in society.

Cook was born in 1858. Among the first sports he took up was boxing. At his prime he became a keen cyclist – he rode a penny-farthing – and became captain of the West Essex Bicycle Club. He was just 21 when he organised the first county meet of cyclists and, just a few years later, was responsible for the first county cycling championship ever held in England, which consisted of a 5-mile race.

Cook went on to set up the Essex County Cycling and Athletic Association. The annual sports event was dubbed the 'Ascot of Athletics'. Cook was himself also known as 'the pioneer of Essex athletics', as an inscription on his tombstone conveniently informs us.

Cook was also a fine footballer and turned out for Chelmsford FC. He was a centre forward, but it will come as little surprise to discover that he also turned his hand to keeping out the goals as well, becoming the club's goalkeeper. He was involved in the formation of the Essex Football Association and became vice-president of the FA.

If Cook had not been taking part himself, you would have probably found him officiating at athletic or cycling events. He was also a member of Essex County Cricket Club. Even when his legs might have been going, Cook did not give up playing sport, turning his hand to billiards, in which he won many regional titles.

Cook had a real passion for sport and believed it was for all, not just the young and athletic. He was a champion of the beginner and those who had little sporting talent. He died at his Great Baddow home in 1908. His funeral was one of the biggest witnessed in Chelmsford.

His epitaph was a simple, but fitting one: 'He ran well the race that was set before him.'

The grave of Robert Cook at Chelmsford cemetery.

Lapse from Grace

A game of cricket can last a long time. Few in Chelmsford in the nineteenth century, as is the case today, had the time to watch a complete match. However, when the great W.G. Grace came to town, everyone wanted to see him in action, but few could afford to take a day off work to watch him at the crease.

One individual came up with the answer, or so they thought. Bills were printed with the simple words: 'W.G. Grace is now batting.' The plan was to post the bills throughout town at the moment Grace came to the crease. Fans could then head to the match at Fair Field and watch him in action. Being the celebrated batsman he was, it was assumed he would remain at the crease for a substantial amount of time, as was normally the case, at least long enough for people to witness him hitting the odd boundary or two.

However, former alderman Frederick Spalding, who in old age published a book on his recollections of his younger years, recorded that the bills were never posted around town. On this occasion, W.G. Grace was dismissed too quickly – out first ball, to be precise. However, Grace is believed to have 'graced' Chelmsford on a number of occasions.

Most cricket matches took place at Fair Field, the venue gaining its name from the fact that fairs were also held there during Victorian times. It no longer exists. Of course, Chelmsford has a purpose-built stadium for cricket these days, the city now home to Essex County Cricket Club. It is situated on the south bank of the River Can overlooking Central Park; a more central city location you would be hard to find. In fact, you can occasionally – if the wind is in the right direction – hear announcements from the stadium during match days as you go about your business in the high street. Don't

The present home of Essex County Cricket Club.

be surprised if the shopkeepers suddenly put a 'closed' sign up and head for the County Ground. It may have just been announced over the loudspeaker that the W.G. Grace of today is on his way to the crease.

Just be quick to get there.

'Willow' Talk

Willow trees growing in the Chelmer Valley and beyond have provided wood for cricket bats for a long time. 'Cricket bat' willows are usually harvested every fifteen to thirty years, with new saplings planted to replace them.

However, one particular tree stands above the rest when it comes to statistics. This giant willow was planted in Boreham in 1835 and allowed to grow until 1888, when it was felled for cricket bat manufacturer Benjamin Warsop. It had grown to a height of more than 100ft. It was said to have measured almost 6ft in diameter and weighed

11 tonnes. Not surprisingly, it was to provide plenty of wood – a total of 1,179 cricket bats, to be precise.

A Two-Horse Town

Galleywood Common, now a haven for wildlife, was once home to one of the country's top racecourses, its meetings attracting thousands of people. Of course, that fact is no secret. The evidence is everywhere, if you take time to look. The village sign depicts racehorses; the names of surrounding pubs have equestrian themes and you can even still see remains of some of the fences the spectators would have stood behind. However, what many Chelmsfordians do not know is that there was once another racecourse on the other side of town. Writtle Races appears to have been a serious rival as well.

A press report of a meeting in 1846 declared: '… there were far greater numbers than we have seen at Galleywood of late years; and probably there were little short of 10,000 people present.' It went on: 'The whole of Oxney Green appeared alive with people.' According to the report, 'excellent musicians … delighted the company with popular airs throughout the day'.

It claimed much of the success of Writtle Races was due to the patronage of Lord Petre, 'the great landowner of the area'. Lady Petre would accompany her husband and the 'socialites of the day followed; to see and be seen'.

The Boy Done Good!

Former Chelmsford City footballer Charlie Hurst did not achieve immortality in the sport. However, his son probably has. Charlie enjoyed many years as a professional footballer, playing for the likes of Bristol Rovers and Oldham Athletic, though it was nothing compared to what son Geoff was to go on to achieve.

But many Chelmsford residents are not even aware that 1966 World Cup winner Geoff Hurst was a Chelmsfordian, if only for a brief period. Hurst famously became the first man to score a hat-trick in a World Cup final, as England defeated West Germany 4–2.

The Hurst family moved to Chelmsford in 1949 when Geoff was 8, and he attended King's Road Primary School. Dad Charlie was near the end of his playing days when he signed for non-league Chelmsford, known as the Clarets, and it was not long before he was on the move again, eventually becoming player-manager of Sudbury Town.

It is certainly not as widely known that Geoff Hurst was also a talented cricketer and played one first-class fixture for Essex CCC in 1962. Ironically, it was against Lancashire, the county of his birth. However, Hurst failed to score a run. He finished on zero not out in his first innings and was then bowled for a duck in the second.

Chelmsford Sign England International

The idea of one of the top Premier League players of today quitting the top flight to play non-league football seems a preposterous one. However, that is what happened in 1909.

Of course, football was not like it is today and it was not all about money in those days. However, it was still a huge shock when Vivian Woodward, at the height of his career, announced his retirement from the top level to play amateur football at Chelmsford.

Woodward, a name few have heard of today, was one of the top players of his time. He signed for Tottenham Hotspur at the beginning of the twentieth century and went on to represent England. He scored an average of more than one goal a game for his country – a record most England strikers of today can only dream about.

Sadly for Chelmsford fans, Woodward did not play many games and, by the end of 1909, he had returned to the big time with Chelsea.

'Come On, City'

Many football fans might be surprised to learn that Chelmsford only became a city in 2012.

The football team has, of course, been bearing the name Chelmsford City since being formed in 1938. It appears the founders were a little ahead of themselves when coming up with a name for the new professional club.

So why was the newly formed club not called Chelmsford Town, for example? The answer remains a mystery. However, it has been suggested that it was a simple mistake and not wishful thinking on the part of the founders. As difficult as it is to believe, it is

Melbourne Park – the current home of Chelmsford City FC.

thought that the founders, on leaving the Golden Fleece public house in Duke Street after agreeing to form a new professional football club, had still not come up with a name for it. They were greeted by the sight of the cathedral and, like many people today, assumed a cathedral was enough to give a place city status. And so Chelmsford 'City' was born, almost seventy-five years too early.

Whatever you wish to believe, football fans in Chelmsford have been chanting 'City' long before the town became one.

Top of the 'Flops'

Thousands of music lovers flock to Chelmsford once a year for the famous V Festival at Hylands Park. Tickets sell out almost as soon as they go on sale. Sadly, one entrepreneur in the 1970s was not so successful in enticing music fans to town, at least on one occasion.

In 1977, Chancellor Hall and the football ground's City Tavern were the two top music venues of the day. Quite a rivalry developed, with both attempting to attract the top bands of the time. Chancellor Hall was the larger venue. It could afford to book the big names.

In an attempt to surpass anything that had taken place at Chancellor Hall, an open-air punk rock festival – a first for Britain – was planned at the football ground in September 1977. Famous DJ and radio presenter John Peel was invited to host the event. The line up included top names, such as The Damned, Eddie and the Hot Rods and Slaughter and the Dogs.

Thousands were expected to attend, but, for a number of reasons, didn't. In fact, just 1,500 turned up. It meant there was not enough money to pay everyone involved. Angry bouncers confronted the organiser backstage and the unfortunate individual had to lock himself in his office, according to a press report. Stewards also walked out. The Damned refused to play and poor John Peel was pelted with bottles and cans by the disgruntled audience. It was a disaster. The show went on to a certain extent, but even the scaffolder started to dismantle the stage area before the concert had ended, with one of the bands still in the middle of their performance at the time.

To make amends for their refusal to play, The Damned did play a later gig free of charge in the town – though the venue chosen probably only rubbed salt into the wound for the organisers of the doomed punk festival. Yes, you guessed it … Chancellor Hall.

There was at least one other unusual music venue in town in the 1970s – the prison. The Sex Pistols performed to inmates in 1976 and recorded an album, *Live at Chelmsford Top Security Prison*, within its walls.

The Man Who Was Always Centre Stage

Wilson Barrett was a man that knew how to draw an audience. And yet mention his name in Chelmsford today and it will most probably only attract a blank stare or the shake of the head. Most today are oblivious to the fact that Barrett was a leading light of his time and arguably one of the most successful Chelmsfordians.

Barrett was an actor, playwright and manager. He is credited with attracting the largest crowds of theatregoers ever. One of his productions – *The Silver King* – was performed to record-breaking audiences and is still regarded as the most successful melodrama of the nineteenth century. The Victorians could not get enough of the work of Barrett and flocked to see him.

Barrett was born at Manor House Farm, Chelmsford, in 1846. His father was an unsuccessful farmer and was forced to move the family to London in search of work.

Wilson Barrett began his professional acting career at

the Theatre Royal in Halifax in 1864. He was not content to stick to acting and later went on to manage that particular establishment.

Barrett also managed a number of London theatres during his career, including the Princess's Theatre, where he put on *The Silver King* in 1882. It was his first big success. The rights of the play were sold abroad and it is said Barrett made a profit of almost £10,000, a huge figure at the time.

Despite this success, Barrett often found himself in debt and was forced to tour the United States to earn enough money to repay his creditors. His second big break came during one of those tours. In 1895, Barrett staged a religious play that he had himself penned. *The Sign of the Cross* proved to be a massive hit and was soon drawing in huge audiences in London as well. It enabled Barrett to settle all his debts, but it was to be his last major achievement: he never again enjoyed the same sort of success. *The Sign of the Cross* was made into a successful film in 1932, long after his death. The biblical epic – produced by Paramount, and starring the likes of Fredric March and Charles Laughton – was based on Barrett's original play. *The Silver King* had also made it on to the big screen, in 1929, but never enjoyed the same sort of success, it being a silent film.

Barrett was an attractive stage personality. He was not a tall man, but there was a presence about him and he had a fine voice. He took the leading roles in a number of Shakespeare's plays, but his interpretation of the characters was often radical. It was said that as the title character in *Hamlet*, Barrett delivered his lines as though the play was a middle-class melodrama, that particular genre always being his first love.

Furthermore, Barrett was a canny manager. At a time

when many fellow managers considered it vulgar to publicise their plays, Barrett recognised the importance of publicity and used it to good effect. He knew how to attract a crowd.

Wilson Barrett may no longer be a household name, or even a familiar one in Chelmsford, but there is little doubt that he made a huge impact in the theatre. His religious plays attracted people that had never set foot in a theatre before and gave the cinema material for one of its greatest biblical epics.

People

Great Scott! Strutt Was Not Only an Olympic Inspiration

It is perhaps fitting that Joseph Strutt now lies at rest almost within the shadow of the enormous Olympic Stadium in London. There are some who might say that if it was not for this now almost forgotten antiquarian and engraver, who was born in Chelmsford in 1749 and buried in Holborn following his death in 1802, the 2012 Olympic Games might never have taken place. That might be stretching the imagination a bit far, but Strutt can probably claim at least some small part in its success.

Strutt was responsible for penning a number of books during his day. He devoted himself to antiquarian research and published illustrated works that were often the first in their field. However, though considered important at the time, none would really set the pulse racing today. *The Regal and Ecclesiastical Antiquities of England* was his first effort, published in 1773, and the first book of its kind, containing a series of engraved portraits. However, his most enduring book is *The Sports and Pastimes of the People of England*, which first appeared in 1801. It is looked upon with interest today, for it contains the history and rules of many of our favourite sporting activities and pursuits. What most people do not know, however, is that the work also influenced the revival of the modern Olympic Games. At the time of its publication, some still considered sport and many pastimes to be inventions of the Devil. The work documented the conflict between religion and popular culture.

The book became an inspiration to a man named William Penny Brookes and helped persuade him to start the Wenlock Olympian Games in 1850. Brookes believed that physical exercise was vital to peoples' well-being. He oversaw a lifelong campaign to get PE on the school curriculum. His interest in the subject led him to the company of Pierre de Coubertin, a Frenchman now deemed to be the 'father of the modern Olympic Games'. In 1890, Coubertin visited Much Wenlock in Shropshire, the home of Brookes. A 'Games' was staged especially for the visitor and, inspired by the event and further discussion with Brookes himself, Coubertin went on to set up the International Olympic Committee in 1894, which was followed by the Athens Olympics two years later.

Of course, Strutt cannot claim he was the sole inspiration for the Olympic Games, though it is not his only claim to fame – a fame this former pupil of King Edward VI Grammar School (one of the four houses there is named after him) – perhaps never really achieved through his own books. However, he at least had a hand in helping another gain fame and fortune, for Strutt can claim some of the credit for the historical novels of Sir Walter Scott. Indeed, if it had not been for Strutt, Scott might never have got round to penning the likes of *Ivanhoe* and becoming one of the country's most celebrated novelists.

When Strutt died in 1802 he left unfinished *Queen-Hoo Hall*, an historical and romantic novel he had been working on. Scott was asked by his publisher to finish it.

Scott was already earning a reputation as a fine poet, but had not yet penned any of the novels that were to make his name all over the world. *Queen-Hoo Hall* was set during the reign of Henry VI, and the book was published in 1808, after Scott added a final chapter. It was not a commercial success. However, in finishing the work of another, Scott was encouraged to conclude a novel of his own that he had consigned to the drawer of his writing desk many years earlier. The work was to become *Waverley*. In the 1829 general preface to *Waverley* – a work that first appeared in 1814 – Scott suggested the novel would not have seen the light if he had not been asked to edit the work of Strutt. He said *Queen-Hoo Hall* 'evinced (in my opinion) considerable powers of imagination'.

Scott believed *Queen-Hoo Hall* failed because Strutt

Springfield Mill – the former home of Joseph Strutt.

displayed his antiquarian knowledge 'too liberally'. Strutt was too preoccupied in highlighting the manners and customs of the time, at the expense of the plot. Scott said: 'I conceived it possible to avoid this error; and, by rendering a similar work more light and obvious to general comprehension, to escape the rock on which my predecessor was shipwrecked.'

Academics remember Strutt as the first serious historian of dress in England and among the first to view visual material in books as being not merely illustrative, but informative and a valuable historical source. Of course, that is not really enough to excite the average man on the street today. Strutt may not be remembered by the masses for his own work, but he was clearly a man of inspiration.

And, even if few give the blue plaque on the wall of his birthplace at Springfield Mill a second glance or have any idea what this son of a wealthy miller achieved through his work, they should perhaps give him a little thought the next time they are whizzing past the Olympic Stadium on the Central Line of the London Underground, or alighting at Edinburgh Waverley railway station.

All at Sea

'England expects that every man will do his duty.' And the man who helped coin that famous phrase during the Battle of Trafalgar expected every woman to do hers as well. Certainly, John Pasco, signal officer to Lord Nelson on HMS *Victory*, felt it was his eldest daughter's duty to be by his side when he went to sea in later years. It meant much of her early life was spent on the ocean waves.

Horatia was born in 1808, some three years after Nelson had defeated the French and lost his own life. Pasco named his daughter in honour of the admiral. Soon after her birth, Horatia was at sea with her father when Pasco was appointed to serve HMS *Hindostan*. In fact, it was not uncommon for a naval captain to take his wife and children with him, despite the obvious dangers. Pasco and Horatia sailed to Australia and, on the return journey, were joined by the governor of New South Wales – the disgraced Captain William Bligh of HMS *Bounty* fame. Horatia may have known little about the voyage, but it was an eventful start to her 'career' at sea.

As for Pasco, her father, he returned to the *Victory* at the end of his career, becoming its first commanding officer at her permanent berth in Portsmouth. He was promoted to rear admiral on the retired list in 1847 and died some six years later.

However, Pasco will forever be remembered as the man who helped Nelson with his famous battle cry. Nelson ordered Pasco to signal to his fleet the words 'England confides that every man will do his duty'. Pasco suggested he substitute 'expects' for 'confides' since the former was already part of the signal vocabulary. It would have taken more time to spell out the letters of 'confides'. Nelson is said to have replied: 'That will do, Pasco, make it directly.' The signal – Nelson's last – has gained immortality.

As for Horatia, she (unsurprisingly) married a naval officer and that is the reason why she became associated with Chelmsford. Husband John Bunch Bonnemaison McHardy was himself taken to sea by Pasco before he reached his teenage years. It is more than probable the couple had met as children on the ocean waves before later falling in love. However, when the couple tied the knot in 1830, Horatia was able to 'retire' from her own naval career. It was no longer considered the norm for wives to be in service at sea with their husbands, and so Horatia stayed at home to raise their large family. The couple, who were to eventually settle in Springfield, were to have many children, a number of whom followed in the footsteps of their father and grandfather – not to mention their mother – in pursuing a naval career.

A Policeman's Lot Is (Sometimes) Not a Happy One

John Bunch Bonnemaison McHardy was to become the first chief constable when Essex Police was founded in 1840. Of course, it is no secret that this once celebrated naval officer, who rose to the rank of admiral, gave up his life on the ocean waves, then 38, for this quite different role. What is perhaps not known is that McHardy himself admitted, prior to taking up his new position, that he had never even set foot in Essex before! However, by all accounts, his appointment was a successful one and he served his newly adopted county with pride.

Having joined the navy at such a young age, McHardy had already enjoyed a long and fruitful career at sea. It is quite possible that McHardy was a family man at heart and had had enough of being parted from wife Horatia – the daughter of John Pasco – and children for long periods. On arrival in Chelmsford, the McHardys first took up residence in King Street until moving to lodgings at the new police headquarters at Old Court, Arbour Lane.

The achievements of McHardy as the chief of police have been much documented. He served the county for more than forty years in the role. And, perhaps fittingly, he and his family are buried at Holy Trinity church, close to their home and within the shadow of Chelmsford Prison.

There is no doubt that McHardy, with so many children, would have enjoyed a rich family life. However, it was not without tragedy. Of course, in those days, many children died of natural causes, though the McHardys were to lose one of their daughters in the most awful of circumstances. If you seek out the family memorial at Holy Trinity church you will find an Emily Gace on it, a name that is most deserving of being there. She was a governess who gave her life for one of her charges.

In 1844, 11-year-old Mary and a younger sister were walking along the River Chelmer, accompanied by 19-year-old Emily. It is believed they were throwing sticks into the water when Mary fell in. Emily jumped in after her, but was unable to save her, and lost her own life in the process. Both were pulled from the water, but nothing could be done. McHardy himself was among those to try in vain to resuscitate his daughter.

McHardy must have been devastated by the loss. It was a cruel way to lose a member of his family. No doubt he had witnessed many friends lose their lives during his earlier career and would never have dreamed he would see anyone else drown – especially someone so close – now that he had given up his life at sea.

J.B.B. McHardy as depicted on a pub sign.

Grand Designs

It is common knowledge that famous landscape designer Humphry Repton had more than a hand in redesigning the gardens at Hylands House. However, it is not so well advertised that his eldest son also left his mark in the city, but through bricks and mortar.

John Adey Repton was an architect by profession and designed Holy Trinity church, Springfield. He was to work with his father on many occasions. While Humphry was busy 'gardening' at a country house, John would often carry out improvements and alterations to the property itself. However, his own career was always hindered by the fact he was deaf from an early age, which meant he found it difficult to deal with clients.

It is perhaps appropriate that Holy Trinity church is today viewed as one of John's greatest achievements, as Springfield became his home until his death in 1860. He moved here with his sister following the death of his parents and died unmarried.

The church designed by John Adey Repton.

John was also an antiquarian. He was associated with Chelmsford Philosophical Society and its museum, donating artefacts. As a writer, he privately printed the intriguing *Some Account of the Beard and the Moustachio, Chiefly from the Sixteenth to the Eighteenth Century* in 1839.

Sadly, John Adey Repton never quite emulated the fame of his father, but he certainly left his mark in Chelmsford, even if few are aware of the fact.

The Tragedy of a Devoted Daughter

The father of Ellen Louisa Pash gained recognition as a great man in Chelmsford during Victorian times, even if he too is little remembered today. However, her mother must have been a wonderful woman too. The young Ellen certainly thought so and her devotion to Mrs Pash resulted in a truly tragic event.

Ellen was the daughter of engineer Joseph Brittain Pash. He was the founder of the successful Essex Industrial School. This establishment evolved out of the home for destitute boys that he founded in 1872. The Essex Home School, as it later became known, began life in two converted houses in Great Baddow. It had just two pupils when it opened. In the following year, it was officially certified as an industrial school and, as a result, numbers grew. Industrial schools were seen as the answer to juvenile delinquency; the idea was to remove problem children from the streets and away from a life of crime. Destitute and neglected boys, particularly orphans, were trained in industrial works in the hope they would have a chance of finding employment in this field. The school accepted disorderly juveniles sent by magistrates, or at least those that were lucky enough to have escaped prison. As the establishment grew, a purpose-built school was constructed at Rainsford End to cater for up to 150 boys. It remained open as a school until 1980.

Boys were taught a variety of trades, including gardening, building, shoemaking, carpentry and engineering. The school would do its utmost to secure its students a job when it was time for them to leave, many finding positions as far away as Australia, New Zealand and Canada.

Ellen took great interest in her father's school. She would herself lecture the boys on all sorts of subjects and continued to correspond with them once they had moved on. Eventually becoming a student herself, Ellen moved to Bangor in Wales to study there. And it was in Wales that she was to meet her death in tragic circumstances.

Ellen's mother was visiting her, but became gravely ill. When Ellen went to her room one morning, she found Mrs Pash lying unconscious in a pool of blood. Ellen feared the worst. The devoted daughter, 'thrown off her balance by this sad sight and thinking that her mother was dead', fled the house and hailed a cab. She ordered the cab driver to take her to the Menai Suspension Bridge that leads to the Isle of Anglesey. There she ascended the high tower and threw herself to her death. Her brother had given chase in another cab, but was too late to prevent the tragedy. He arrived just in time to witness the fatal fall. It is believed to have been the first incident of its sort at the bridge.

In fact, Mrs Pash was not dead. She had merely broken a blood vessel.

A press report of the incident in 1903 sensitively summed up the tragedy: 'Painful as it was, it [the death of Ellen] arose from the most beautiful and touching of all causes – a daughter's tender affection for a good mother whose life she erroneously believed had suddenly ended.'

Sadly, Mrs Pash died herself in the following year.

A Question of Freedom

Who was the first freeman of Chelmsford? Ask that question and few Chelmsfordians will have the faintest idea. However, it would make a great question for a pub quiz at one particular hostelry in the city – the Sir Evelyn Wood at Widford. And shame on the punters if they failed to get the answer right, for Field Marshal Sir Evelyn Wood, in whose honour the pub is named, was that very man.

Sir Evelyn Wood depicted on a sign at a pub named in his honour.

Wood, a military hero during Victorian times, received the freedom of Chelmsford in 1903 to commemorate his elevation to the rank of field marshal. As early as 1879, he was presented with a Sword of Honour at Shire Hall, in recognition of his services to the country.

Wood was the son of the vicar of Cressing. He joined the navy in his early teens. However, he discovered he was better suited to land warfare and transferred to the army. As a cavalry officer, Wood played a major part in suppressing the Indian Rebellion of 1857 and native uprisings in South Africa. He was awarded the Victoria Cross for rescuing a local merchant from a band of robbers during the former conflict.

Wood was also a successful author, penning a number of military works. He died in 1919.

Only a Slave for Christ in the End

One could argue that Sir Evelyn Wood was not actually the first freeman of Chelmsford. That title should perhaps go to a man named Joseph. Indeed, his friends gave it to him, at the very least. He was to them – as his gravestone informs us – Joseph 'Free Man'.

That title would have certainly had more relevance and significance to Joseph than the likes of Evelyn Wood or anyone else granted certain privileges on receiving the freedom of a city or town.

Joseph was a slave in New Orleans who escaped and made his way to England to begin a new life. Nothing much else is known about him. The manner of his escape is a mystery and it is not known how he ended up in Chelmsford. He had a large family and attended Ebenezer Chapel in New London Road. His gravestone in the Non-Conformist cemetery in that same street informs us that he worked at the London Road ironworks until his death at the age of 45 in 1875.

The grave of Joseph, a former slave.

Apart from gaining his freedom from slavery, Joseph also became a 'Free Man' in Christ, his 'Christian friends' inform us on the inscription. They must have been fond of Joseph to go to such trouble to remember him. Certainly, they would have seen his experiences and life as symbolic to the Christian faith. The inscription warns: 'Reader! Have you been made free from the slavery of sin?'

Showing People in Their True Colours

You will find many black and white photographs of old Writtle taken before the First World War, like you would of any place in Britain. However, you can even find some colour ones. And that is something most places cannot claim. In fact, it is believed that a Writtle resident was responsible for taking Britain's first colour photograph using the autochrome process.

Thomas Usborne was a brewer and former MP for Chelmsford. He lived in an enormous house adjacent to the old Writtle brewery, both his home and that business having since been demolished. Usborne married the daughter of the brewery and went on to become director of the business. He owned a vast amount of land, his estate even boasting its own gasworks. Towards the end of the nineteenth century, it is recorded that he had more than a dozen indoor servants.

Colour photography was still in its infancy at the beginning of the twentieth century. The Lumière brothers first marketed autochrome, the process through which colour photographs were first produced, in 1907. And it was mostly thanks to the humble potato. The process involved millions of microscopic grains of potato starch, dyed in shades of red, green and violet, being compressed with a roller over a glass plate. The plate was then exposed to light, the grains acting as filters and revealing a colour image. Colour photography had been explored throughout the nineteenth century, but the early pioneers struggled to create permanent images. The autochrome process remained the main process for producing colour photographs until the introduction of colour film in the mid-1930s.

Autochrome plates first went on sale in Britain in 1907. Usborne was by then a very rich man and could afford what would have then been an expensive and time-consuming hobby; each plate would have taken about twelve hours to process. Usborne made numerous stereoscopic colour plates, his garden and trips abroad the focus of most of his attention.

Usborne, an Irishman, lived in Writtle for most of his life. He died in 1915 and is buried in the village church. One of his other claims to fame is that he was also one of the early pioneers of the game of bridge.

Have I Got News for You

Chelmsfordians who read a particular national newspaper are probably blissfully unaware they do so thanks to a former resident.

The man who brought the nation the *Daily Express* in 1900 was the son of a Springfield rector. He was not only a very successful newspaper proprietor, however. His concern for the less fortunate – particularly the blind – made him a man that the city of Chelmsford can look upon with much pride. Sadly, very few residents today will have even heard of the name Sir Arthur Pearson.

Parishioners at All Saints church in Springfield should have at least some knowledge of Arthur's father, though. Revd Pearson served as rector for many years and was very popular. Though Arthur himself did not stay long in Chelmsford – soon moving away to study – his formative years were spent here.

The meteoric rise of Arthur Pearson started in 1884, when he won a competition set up by George Newnes – the founder of *Tit-Bits* magazine. The prize was a clerkship at the magazine's London office. Pearson took up his position with relish and, by the following year, had been promoted to manager. He was only 20 when he effectively became the right-hand man of the influential Newnes. But that was still not good enough for the ambitious Pearson. In 1890, he decided to go it alone and set up his own business, issuing his own publication – *Pearson's Weekly*.

All Saints church, Springfield.

The aim of the periodical journal was 'to interest, to elevate, to amuse'. It contained plenty of articles and stories, but the secret of its success was its innovative guessing games. When the publication was struggling to attract readers, Pearson introduced a 'missing word' competition. Readers loved it. It became the turning point in his career and made him a fortune. Sales of the magazine reached a peak of more than 1.25 million in 1897. In 1900, Pearson launched a daily newspaper, which is still on our stands today – the *Daily Express*.

Some four years later, he acquired the *Standard* and *Evening Standard*. However, from about 1910, Pearson started to relinquish his newspaper holdings and made a decision to devote his life to a quite different cause. He became president of the National Institute for the Blind, something close to his heart. Pearson had started to lose his own sight in about 1908, having suffered poor eyesight all his life. He became affectionately known as the 'blind leader of the blind' and did much to change the public perception of blind people in a positive way.

Pearson was created a baronet in 1916 in recognition of his work for the blind. Among the success stories was St Dunstan's, an establishment in which soldiers blinded during the war could learn a trade and therefore remain independent.

Pearson helped many causes in his role as a philanthropist. Less well known than his work for the blind was his desire to help children from difficult backgrounds. He would fund trips to the countryside for youngsters from the slums who had never even seen a cow before. He can also claim a part in the formation of the Scout movement. Pearson was a loyal supporter of Robert Baden-Powell's initiative and published the landmark handbook *Scouting for Boys*, as well as a regular magazine for the movement. It is therefore quite appropriate that Chelmsford – Hylands Park to be precise – was chosen as the venue for the 21st World Scout Jamboree in 2007, which celebrated the centenary of Scouting.

The Lion King

You are unlikely to find many lion tamers in Chelmsford these days, so it is perhaps a surprise that George Newcomb is not remembered today. He was not only Chelmsford's most famous lion tamer, but, apparently, one of the most famous in the world.

Newcomb was born in Chelmsford in the 1830s. He joined the circus as a teenager, initially cleaning out cages. By his own admission, he got to know the animals and, most importantly, found out which ones he could trust. It was not long before he was not bothering to get the animals out of the cages before he started to clean them. He would think nothing of sharing a cage with a lion.

Newcomb travelled with Wombwell's, the most famous of Victorian menageries, becoming a celebrated lion tamer. He performed all over the world and earned a fine reputation. During one performance it is said he entered a den occupied by four lions, two wolves, two hyenas and two bears. No doubt, they were too busy fighting each other to worry about Newcomb!

Of course, things did not always go according to plan and Newcomb did sustain many injuries during his career. A dispute with a leopard resulted in the loss of one of his eyes, and he nearly lost his life when he was attacked while performing with five lions during one particular performance. His injuries were so bad that Newcomb was forced to return to his home in Broomfield Road for six months in order to recuperate.

However, Newcomb eventually became bored with his life as a lion tamer – and gave it up for the thrilling life of a carpenter.

The Lord of the Manor Who Was Left Out of Pocket

Famous poet and translator Alexander Barclay left a small sum of money in his will to the poor of Great Baddow following his death. However, he should have perhaps left something for the lord of the manor too.

John Paschall put Barclay up when the latter initially came to serve the parish as rector in 1549. Presumably, the rectory was not at the time fit for a renowned scribe, who had already penned, in the early part of the sixteenth century, the satirical poem 'The Ship of Fools', which earned him a place among the greats of English literature.

Barclay became known as the Black Monk or Black Poet, having worn the habit, first at Ely, and then at Canterbury. He was already serving the more prosperous benefice of Wookey in Somerset when he came to Great Baddow as rector, on the presentation of Paschall.

Famous scribe Alexander Barclay was a former rector of Great Baddow.

He was allowed to keep the former position, presumably by hiring a curate to see to the everyday needs of his Wookey parishioners. It is said Barclay paid Paschall money for the rebuilding of the rectory at Great Baddow, initially lodging with him for a few months, presumably while the work was being carried out.

But, in 1554, some two years after the death of Barclay, Paschall was suing his rector's executors for what he claimed were further unpaid costs of the project. It is said Barclay died a wealthy man, due to his two livings, but it appears he might not have been as liberal with his money as he should have been.

Metals and Petals

You are unlikely to find the name Robert Warner in a history book on Chelmsford. However, you might find it in one on botany. This little-remembered hydraulic engineer and bell founder had a 'softer' side – a love of orchids – and even gave his name to one.

Warner's hobby could not have been more different to the day job. His firm designed and constructed pumping machinery for waterworks and mines. It also produced bells that were hung all over the world, being the firm responsible for the first bell at the Houses of Parliament.

But Warner's real love was orchids. His successful business life earned him much wealth and he could afford to indulge in his passion. It is said Warner was once in possession of the finest collection of orchids in the world. He became an expert on orchids and from Scravels, his Broomfield home, wrote much on the subject, including the book *Select Orchidaceous Plants*, which was first published in 1862. It is in that work that Warner pictured four lavender flowers under the name 'Cattleya warneri', which he claimed was a new species.

Warner spent much of his life in Chelmsford, later moving to Widford Lodge.

The Mystery Admiral

Few know much or indeed anything about the admiral who gave his name to one of the most popular green spaces in Chelmsford. Central Park, as the name suggests, sits at the heart of the city centre. It flows almost seamlessly into Admiral's Park, named after Rear Admiral John Faithful Fortescue.

So what did this sailor do to earn this honour? The answer is simply that he once owned the land here, and it was not because of some heroic action at sea.

Rear Admiral John Faithful Fortescue.

However, that is not to say Fortescue did not distinguish himself during his career on the high seas. The fact he was promoted to superannuated rear admiral following his retirement is perhaps evidence he served his country well.

The truth is that there is not a lot known about Fortescue, despite the position he reached after serving the navy for what is thought to have been more than twenty-five years. It has led to him being dubbed the 'mystery admiral' by many today.

Fortescue was in his mid-twenties when he became a lieutenant and then, in 1781, was promoted commander of HMS *Lightning*. He took control of another fireship – the *Incendiary* – in the following year, before becoming a captain. It is thought he then served at least one other ship, but, from the mid-1780s, there appears to be no record of his service until he was promoted to rear admiral on the retired list in 1805. Those intervening years appear to be something of a mystery, but the fact the Admiralty honoured him at the beginning of the nineteenth century – in the year of the Battle of Trafalgar to be precise – suggests he was still very much in its thoughts.

Fortescue obtained Writtle Lodge, which was built in 1712, as part of a dowry. Sadly, the mansion no longer stands, but part of Fortescue's vast estate was eventually converted into a public park towards the end of the nineteenth century, it having remained in the family following his death in 1819. And so Admiral's Park remains to this day open for all to enjoy and is perhaps a fitting name, if only for the fact an important naval officer once resided here, his adventures at sea still largely a mystery.

A Different View of Things

We all like a room with a view. Indeed, many homebuyers turn down properties they love simply because the view from the house is not to their taste.

The view from Hylands House was apparently not to the taste of John Attwood when he moved here in 1839. However, he had no intention of looking elsewhere for his dream home and instead set about improving the outlook from his new abode. Attwood, who was not short of a shilling or two, proceeded to purchase all the properties surrounding his estate. Then he demolished them. Writtle Lodge, a grand mansion itself, was one of a number of houses that he viewed to be a blot on the landscape.

As well as removing all properties within view, Attwood also built a perimeter wall around his enlarged estate – presumably he could still see over it from his house. He also bought from the parish the right to stop up part of the public highway near his home, paying £1,000 in 'compensation'. The estate was increased from 750 to 4,300 acres, though it is no longer that size today.

Attwood, who made his fortune in the iron industry, was not afraid to spend money in order to get what he wanted. As an MP, he lost his seat in the House of Commons when he was found guilty of election bribery. He spent thousands of pounds paying the electors of Harwich for their votes.

Attwood owned Hylands House for fifteen years, but his extravagant ways caught up with him. He fell into debt and was forced to sell his Widford estate. He ended his life in poverty and died in France.

Close to the Bone

Writers know you have to add the flesh to the bones in order to compile a good story. Diarist Dr John Henry Salter had no need to on one occasion, though. In fact, it was the lack of flesh in this particular instance that made it such a good story.

Salter was a physician by trade. However, he was also an Essex eccentric who travelled the world in search of thrills. He was a top bare-knuckle fighter and famously, having no suitable trousers to wear at the time, went hunting for bears in the snows of Russia wearing his pyjamas. Needless to say, Salter lived life to the full and he was not short of a good anecdote. Fortunately, he kept a diary from the age of 8 until his death in his 91st year, penning more than 10 million words.

It was as a medical student that Salter came to Chelmsford for the November Fair in 1874. Sadly, freak shows were part of the entertainment in those days. Being a medical chap, Salter was particularly interested in a 'skeleton man' being exhibited. He paid his 2*d* and confronted the form of a skeleton behind a screen. Salter said women were swooning at the mere glimpse of the grinning silhouette and men were quick to make their exit for fear they would hit the ground too, such was the ghoulish and unexplained sight that greeted them.

Salter was naturally suspicious and stepped forward in an attempt to have a closer examination of the figure behind the screen. As he did so, the manager of the show confronted him. However, the manager, on being informed that Salter was a doctor, permitted his suspicious visitor to examine the man in private. Salter was surprised to find it was no trick. The skeleton man had no hair on his body and he had nothing but skin over his bones – no perceivable muscles. However, he had no problem standing, and it is said he could even run and jostle with a fat boy who also performed with the company. Salter wrote: 'This ghoul-like mortal ails nothing. He eats, drinks, smokes, sleeps, takes exercise, and shows fits of temper and intelligence. He is said to have never had a day's illness in his life, to be capable of drinking alcoholic drinks in somewhat large quantities;

and the only faculties which appear to be defective are his hearing and speech.'

Robert, the name of the skeleton man, was just 4ft 6in in height and weighed 49lbs, according to Salter. He measured 27in round the chest and barely 3in round the wrist. Salter concluded: 'He actually was a bona fide man with a skeleton over which was a drawn a skin.'

The manager of the show was of the belief that his skeleton man only had to make himself known to the general public to gain instant fame. He was right. Salter sent the man to the College of Surgeons. All sorts of experiments were carried out on him and he travelled widely for several years, becoming the fascination of medical experts throughout the country, and earning a considerable amount of money for his troubles.

The Height of His Career

It is fair to say Frederick Post reached great heights. However, few in Chelmsford today will know the name.

Chelmsford was once home to two very distinctive landmarks – a pair of wireless masts that both reached a height of some 450ft. The masts were located in the grounds of the Marconi Company's factory in New Street, which was established in 1912.

As foreman of the mast riggers, Post had the job of carrying out repairs, a task few would have relished. He took it upon himself to climb the masts on occasions. There are stories of him climbing – unaided – to the very top by merely putting his feet on the bolt heads.

The masts towered over the town until 1935. When they were taken down, workers took some of the large bolts home with them to keep as unusual souvenirs. No doubt you might still find the odd one or two throughout homes in Chelmsford today, holding open a door or propping up some books.

The Marconi Company's factory in New Street was once home to two giant masts.

Miscellaneous

It Doesn't Just Rain ...

It was not only rain that fell in Chelmsford during the fateful summer of 1888 – but snow as well. The summer of that year will forever be remembered for the floods of July and August that left the town and surrounding area under several feet of water. At the end of July, more than 4in of rain fell in five days. It caused major flooding, the worst Chelmsford has ever witnessed, at least in modern times.

Many properties were destroyed or damaged, not only by floodwater, but by lightning, which also killed many farm animals. Cattle drowned as well. The rivers overflowed and water surged through the town. The iron bridge over the River Can at New London Road was

Snow is usually restricted to the winter months these days.

swept away. Even the stone bridge, which still stands today, swayed and cracked.

The police were, predictably, very busy with the rescue operation under the command of their chief constable. His name? Edward Showers.

Of course, much has been written about the Great Flood of 1888, though what is not so well known is that that particular summer was not only a wet one, but an extremely cold one as well. On 11 July – supposedly the height of summer – there were reports of snow on the outskirts of Chelmsford and elsewhere in the county. As you can imagine, it was not exactly a summer for short sleeves and cricket. Indeed, the cricket season – due to so many postponements – did not conclude until well into the autumn.

Essex is officially the driest county in England, but it seems that when it rains, it pours … and snows!

Mary, Mary …

Few people heading past Chelmsford Cathedral stop to read the inscription on a memorial in the churchyard dedicated to 'three unfortunate females'. It barely receives a glance in today's fast-moving world.

The inscription on the tomb laments the death of three women – all killed during the 'Late Deplorable Fire' of 1808. That particular fire was a major incident in the history of the town, with a large part of Chelmsford destroyed by the flames.

However, the memorial reveals a bizarre fact. The three victims of the house where the fire started – a milliner and her two apprentices – all shared the name Mary. And, now, sadly, the 'three unfortunate females', as a pamphlet issued after the event labelled them, share the same tomb, having been 'hurried into eternity by the awful fire which visited this town on the morning of the nineteenth of March 1808'.

The memorial dedicated to 'three unfortunate females' who share a
tomb and something else.

The memorial also warns others to be on their guard.
The gloomy advice the inscription offers is: 'Prepare for
death ere ye retire to rest. For ye know not what a day
may bring forth.'

Who Knows Where All The Bodies Are Buried?

The first decade of the nineteenth century was not a good one for Chelmsford, as far as fires go. The 'Late Deplorable Fire' was preceded by another tragedy some four years earlier. But, if few are aware of the memorial to the 'three unfortunate females' of the 1808 disaster, even fewer will be aware of the existence of a grave in the same churchyard that holds the remains of thirteen Hanoverians, also victims of a major blaze.

And what is so tragic about this incident is that the deaths of the unlucky thirteen might have been prevented if at least one of the foreigners had known how to unfasten a stable door.

Apparently around seventy Hanoverian troops – the party also made up of women – were forced to sleep in a stable at the long-gone Spotted Dog in what is now Tindal Street. The town was already so full of soldiers that there was no room at the inn for the newcomers when they arrived in Chelmsford that October evening.

The stable door was not locked, merely fastened on the outside by a latch. To lift the latch from within, one had to poke their finger through a hole in the door. Of course, presumably no one had bothered to tell the foreigners that and, probably being unfamiliar with that type of fastening, they believed the door to be locked when fire broke out in the stable. The cries of the 'trapped' occupants were eventually heard, but too late for thirteen of them.

All thirteen – in separate coffins – were buried in one enormous grave in the parish churchyard, a huge mound once marking their resting place. A suitable stone memorial with an inscription dedicated to the thirteen – 'names unknown' – was later added, but time has since eroded that visible reminder and few who now take a stroll among the gravestones are aware of exactly what lies beneath.

And Another Mr and Mrs Smith

The village of Sandon on the outskirts of Chelmsford might have become a major tourism destination if clergymen at the parish church had followed in the footsteps of Revd Gilbert Dillingham. Gretna Green, just over the English border in Scotland, has become legendary as a place for 'shotgun' weddings. However, Essex once had its own 'Gretna Green' thanks to the Revd Dillingham.

Dillingham came to Sandon as rector of St Andrew's church at the beginning of the seventeenth century. For many years, he was asked to officiate at no more than a handful of weddings a year, the parish not being overpopulated. However, in about 1615, the forward-thinking Dillingham came up with a novel way of making some money. Virtually overnight, Sandon became known as a place to get married, no questions asked. Eloping couples, or those in need of a 'shotgun' wedding, headed for St Andrew's church.

The village of Sandon might have been very different if the ways of a former rector had taken off.

It is said that hundreds of runaway brides from far and wide turned up on Dillingham's doorstep. While clergymen of the day would have been horrified at the suggestion of being asked to marry couples without ensuring they met all the requirements of the Church, Dillingham appeared to be happy to do the honours – for the right fee, of course. Couples used false names and Dillingham, it appears, did not even raise an eyebrow to the fact that there would, no doubt, have been quite a lot of happy couples bearing the name 'Smith'.

Revd Dillingham is believed to have officiated at more than 500 weddings. It is said he even married the daughter of a vicar from a neighbouring parish.

Gretna Green did not become a wedding destination until 1754 and so Dillingham was well ahead of his time. However, the rector that replaced Dillingham at Sandon in the mid-1630s had no intention of continuing the venture and so Sandon did not become what Gretna Green is today. It is said that Dillingham's replacement was turning disappointed couples away from his doorstep for many years.

Your Wish Is My Command

It was within a Chelmsford coaching inn – still standing today – that two clergymen prompted a man to bump off one of the most familiar 'celebrities' of mid-Victorian England.

The Saracen's Head was a regular haunt of novelist Anthony Trollope, a one-time resident of Waltham Cross on the Hertfordshire-Essex border. It is thought his work as a Post Office official and love of hunting took him to the county town of Essex on numerous occasions. His novels, like those of many leading writers of the day, appeared in monthly or weekly instalments. They were the soap operas of the time.

Murder was once plotted at the Saracen's Head.

Trollope was supposedly sitting in the smoking room at the Saracen's Head when two men of the cloth entered with the latest instalment of what later became known as Trollope's Barsetshire novels. People would talk about the characters as though they were real people and the scheming Mrs Proudie, still deemed to be one of the most despicable characters in English literature, had at the time become one of the most hated 'celebrities' in mid-Victorian Britain.

One clergyman, speaking to the other, cursed Mrs Proudie and declared: 'I wish she was dead.' Trollope overheard the men and looked up from his table. He is said to have calmly replied: 'Gentlemen, she shall die in the next number.'

And so, true to his word, Trollope freed England from the despicable Mrs Proudie.

Ironically, the author is believed to have met the inspiration for Mrs Proudie at the Essex town of Saffron Walden. So it is only fair that it should be in the county town of Essex that the idea to finish her off was put into his head.

It's Not Farewell to Arms

The history books will tell you that nothing remains of old Moulsham Hall, seat of the Mildmays. That is not strictly true. And you only have to look up for the proof.

Pinned to an outside wall of Chelmsford Museum at Oaklands Park is part of the Mildmay coat of arms that once graced their family home. As people head for the entrance of the museum, it can be easily overlooked and it is surprising just how many have never even noticed it before.

The Mildmay coat of arms.

Those that do know of its existence are probably unaware of the strange circumstances in which it got there, however. The coat of arms was only acquired by the museum in 1963, having been rediscovered built into a wall of a Brentwood motor garage.

Moulsham Hall was demolished at the beginning of the nineteenth century. One of the lions on the coat of arms is missing and only part of the family motto *Alla ta Hara* (God my Help) is now visible.

Bull in a Knick-Knack Shop

No doubt you have heard the term 'bull in a china shop'. And it is a good job Frederick Spalding did not trade in that particular field, for a young bull is exactly what appeared in his high street establishment one day. Fortunately, Spalding was a photographer and did not trade in delicate chinaware, though he did also sell quality knick-knacks and fancy goods, with the result that the beast did still cause a significant amount of damage.

The livestock market was held in Chelmsford's high street until the late nineteenth century, when it was finally moved to a new home behind the now-demolished Corn Exchange. The move was of great benefit to shop owners and innkeepers. One does not have to imagine what market day was like at the time. The mess and smell from the animals would not have been conducive to passing trade or window-shopping. However, cattle continued to be driven through the town until after the Second World War.

Spalding himself noted that it was not unusual for cattle to stray into his shop. On one occasion, a young bull decided to see for himself what was on offer at his Tindal Square premises. However, it was not content to stay on the ground floor, but proceeded to climb the stairs, where upon it entered a sitting room and then the bedroom belonging to two female assistants. Fortunately, that particular chamber was unoccupied at the time.

Photographer Spalding, who in later years penned his recollections as a young man, quipped: 'We were so anxious to get him downstairs – I quite forgot to ask him to give me a sitting.'

It was not the only time an animal ended up in the shop of Spalding. Just before the First World War, a horse and its rider did so, but via the window!

A young boy was asked to take a horse to the yard of the Saracen's Head for shoeing. He was warned not to attempt to ride the horse. However, the temptation proved too much for the youngster and, as he mounted the steed, it bolted. The boy, holding on for dear life, managed to steer it through Duke Street and into Tindal Square towards the Saracen's Head. However, he missed his target; Spalding's shop being adjacent to that particular inn, the horse and boy crashed through his shop window before coming to a halt. The boy was taken to hospital but fortunately lived to tell the tale.

What's Another Year

There should be no doubt as to when the statue of Sir Nicholas Conyngham Tindal – arguably Chelmsford's most famous son – was unveiled. On it is the inscription: 'Erected AD 1850.' However, that is not true. The statue was actually erected in the following year. Of course, few Chelmsfordians today will realise the date is wrong and, to put it bluntly, few would probably care.

It took the local authorities so long to decide where to put Judge Tindal – a whole year to be precise – that by the time a decision was made ... the inscription was out of date. Having taken such care over positioning the statue, it does seem a little strange that they did not feel the need to change the date. Perhaps by then they had

had enough, though there is also the chance they may have hoped no one would actually notice the incorrect date. And, of course, few today do.

Tindal was born in Moulsham Street in 1776 and educated at the King Edward VI Grammar School. He became a celebrated lawyer and won the hearts of the nation for his role in clearing the name of Queen Caroline, the estranged wife of George IV, in what was one of the biggest scandals in royal history. Tindal also became a great reformer and was Lord Chief Justice of Common Pleas from 1829 until his death in 1846. He presided over the trial of a man who, in attempting to assassinate Prime Minister Robert Peel, mistakenly shot and killed his secretary. However, the murderer was seriously mentally ill and was acquitted on the grounds that he did not know what he was doing at the time, the landmark verdict causing a sensation. It led to the now frequently used plea 'not guilty by reason of insanity'. Tindal also introduced the defence (to murder) of provocation.

The nation mourned Judge Tindal on his death and it was no surprise that the people of Chelmsford decided to honour him with a statue. Tindal never forgot his home town and would often return to preside over trials at Shire Hall. It seemed only fitting his memorial should be erected outside that particular building. And that was where it should have been positioned in the autumn of 1850. However, there was concern the new statue would obstruct traffic in the high street. Alternative sites were suggested, but rejected. In the end, it was decided to remove the rotunda over the conduit and erect the statue there; the new position was, at least, within the shadow of Shire Hall. A special base was constructed in order that the water supply from the conduit, which had supplied the town for centuries, should not be affected.

Judge Tindal now takes pride of place opposite Shire Hall.

However, by the summer of 1851, the statue had still not been erected. Many locals were now angered by the fact that the classical rotunda would have to make way for it. A public meeting was held, but the protestors lost out and, finally, in October 1851 – one year late – Sir Nicholas Conyngham Tindal was finally placed into position, a spot he still holds to this day, his memorial being one of the most recognised landmarks in Chelmsford.

As for the conduit rotunda, it was moved up the high street to the junction of Springfield Road, opposite the former Black Boy Inn, where it helped to divide the traffic. It has since found a new home at Tower Gardens in Admiral's Park. In a final victory for Tindal over the conduit rotunda, the name Conduit Square was changed to Tindal Square. The judge still sits proudly in his prominent position at the bottom of the high street, watching over busy shoppers. Of course, few are aware of the fuss to get him there.

The conduit rotunda at its present home in Tower Gardens.

The French Connection

The name Chelmsford can be found throughout the world. However, it is odd that a French-speaking town in Ontario, Canada should have such an English name.

Chelmsford, Ontario was established in the second half of the nineteenth century. French families settled there and many might wonder why it does not bear a French name. A civil engineer from Chelmsford, England is the reason. He was one of three Englishmen working on a new stretch of line for the Canadian Pacific Railway. When the line forked, three names were needed for three new stations. It is said the three engineers named the stations after their home towns, the other two being Romford and Sudbury.

And it is not the first time the French could claim to have been hard done by. They might say Chelmsford in England should be known by something a little more French, for it was a Frenchman – William of St-Mère-Église – who 'founded' the town following the Norman Conquest. William, then Bishop of London, was granted the right to hold a weekly market at 'Chelmersford' in 1199 by King John.

The Odd Fellows

Edmund Durrant was a nineteenth-century bookseller who did his best to make it on to his own shelves. And, in a way, he succeeded, though it was not through writing a best-seller, but by becoming a 'book' himself!

Durrant founded the Chelmsford Odd Volumes. It was a club limited to less than fifty people, with eccentrics like Durrant who shared a passion for literature, art, music, science and archaeology, among other things. Members met at Durrant's house and bookshop in the high street after the select club was formed in 1888. Each member had to be elected to the 'shelf'. The members themselves lectured each other on their own specialist subject, or outside speakers were sometimes invited to talk. Each member was given a unique volume number, Durrant being Volume One. Members could be fined if they did not address fellow members by the volume number given to them on admission to the society, and members were not allowed to answer to anything other than their new title. Those who filled official positions within the club also went by other names. The secretary was known as Honorary Minute Book and the treasurer was called Honorary Cash Book.

There were other Odd Volumes throughout the country and the world. The society was founded in Boston, Massachusetts, in 1887, though the inspiration probably came from The Set of Odd Volumes, an English bibliophile dining-club that was formed in 1878.

Chelmsford was not the first society of Odd Volumes in Britain, but when a set for ladies was formed in the town in 1896, it is thought to have been the first in the country and the whole of the British Empire.

Through the Mill

Rising food prices in our supermarkets today are unlikely to prevent us from carrying out the weekly shop. We may feel the need to cut down on a few non-essential items, but the average man on the street will not go hungry. That was not the case in Chelmsford towards the end of the eighteenth century, however. Inflated food prices at the time meant that many were unable to afford even a loaf of bread.

With fire in their bellies – and little else – a group of poor people from Chelmsford and its neighbouring villages decided to take action. Fed up with shopkeepers making profits at the expense of their customers, the rebels decided to cut out the middlemen. One evening, they marched to Moulsham Mill, where they found a couple of carts loaded with flour ready to be transported to the

Moulsham Mill.

capital. They seized one of the wagons and took it to the market square. Their plan had never been to steal the flour. Instead, they proceeded to sell it at a price they believed was fair and one that the people could afford. They then gave the money to the miller from whom they had obtained the flour.

In the days that followed, the poor and hungry rebels persuaded other millers to sell them flour at that same reduced price they had sold it for in the market. They even approached farmers for the wheat that the millers needed, ensuring the miller got a fair price for it. Butchers were also targeted in this way. Meat being transported was 'commandeered' and sold at a price the poor could afford. Apparently, even the farmers and millers were sympathetic to their plight and generously gave up their goods.

However, the practice eventually came to an end when the rebels were warned by the magistrate that their assembly was illegal, and that he would read the Riot Act if they did not disperse. It is said the rebels had, by this time, also resorted to threatening grocers with weapons in order to get them to lower their prices.

Some of the ringleaders were brought to book, but most deemed it to have generally been a civilised rebellion brought on by necessity. It was certainly better than stealing. Indeed, one perhaps has to admire the way the people stood up to those that they believed were ripping them off. Supermarkets beware!

A Cock and 'Bell' Story

One day in 1768, the landlord of the Cock and Bell Inn at Writtle was possibly trying to explain to a punter that he was hungry. Highly unlikely as it is, that could at least be an explanation as to why he took on the bizarre challenge of trying to race a horse – not by becoming a jockey and riding the steed, but by literally racing against it … on his own two legs.

Perhaps Mr Lambert (the landlord) had just innocently declared: 'I could eat a horse.' Someone may have mistook the word 'eat' for 'beat' and that may explain why the publican found himself sharing the starting line with a horse one day. Whatever the origin of the challenge, there Mr Lambert is said to have found himself and it certainly must have created plenty of interest. It is said there was much betting before the race – presumably in favour of the horse.

However, Mr Lambert only had to run 5 miles before turning back, while the horse had to go 10 miles before returning for home, meaning it had double the distance to run. It still must have been some effort on the part of the master of the Cock and Bell, who is said to have returned home some thirty minutes before his four-legged competitor.

The Cock and Bell Inn is now known as the Blue Bridge restaurant. Perhaps the Cock and 'Bull' Inn would be a better name!

The Mystery Tower

On the outside wall of a row of terraced cottages close to the city centre is a date plaque bearing a bold 3D depiction of a tower. Freston Terrace was the name given to the row of houses in Orchard Street when they were built at the beginning of the twentieth century. And that very name gives more than a hint as to the identity of the tower that the image depicts.

Freston Tower is situated overlooking the River Orwell estuary in neighbouring Suffolk. It was constructed in the sixteenth century, possibly even earlier, though it is not

The mystery tower depicted on the wall of a terrace of cottages in Chelmsford.

known exactly when or why. Historians suggest it could have been built as a lookout for returning ships or merely as an extravagant folly, which, if so, would make it one of the earliest follies in England.

The real tower on which the image is based.

Even more of a mystery is why the tower should be depicted on a row of humble terraced cottages many miles away in Chelmsford. A connection between Freston Tower and the person who produced an image of it on the Orchard Street cottages has yet to be established. So, in the meantime, the full story will have to remain one of many secrets in the history of Chelmsford.

And Finally ... A Few More Snippets

The Wrays – a well-known family of stonemasons in Chelmsford over the decades – had a hand in building the London Monument, which was erected to commemorate the Great Fire of London in 1666.

George Calver set himself up in Chelmsford as a professional telescope maker in the 1860s.

Calver – known as the 'master mirror maker' – is said to have produced thousands of mirrors for telescopes from his Widford premises. He is widely considered the best telescope maker of his time.

Hylands House could have been the location for the University of Essex.

Christine Hanbury – the final private owner of the estate – wanted to leave the property to the public. In the 1950s, a site was being sought for the new university. Hylands Park seemed to be the perfect location for it. However, those making the final decision chose Colchester ahead of the county town. Chelmsford Borough Council eventually bought the estate in the mid-1960s, following the death of Mrs Hanbury.

William Petre, 11th Baron Petre, loved horses.

He was responsible for the racecourse at Oxney Green and, it is reputed, was the man that acquired

Marengo, Napoleon's famous warhorse, following the Battle of Waterloo.

The first home of Chelmsford Museum was in the town prison.

Museum founder Thomas Clarkson Neale also happened to be the governor of the gaol and decided to put his parlour to good use, displaying a number of artefacts there during the 1830s. Chelmsford Museum had a number of homes before moving to its present location in Oaklands Park.

Many Chelmsford inns put on sideshows or exhibited freaks in a bid to lure punters.

The White Lion, which became the Golden Lion, exhibited a young cow towards the end of the eighteenth century. It is said that this particular calf was born with five legs, two tails and two udders.

Chelmsford Museum – now situated in Oaklands Park – had an unusual first home.

Primrose Hill, west of the city centre, does not exactly live up to its name. There is barely a blade of grass to be seen amidst the terraced houses, let alone a primrose.

There may have been flowers here once upon a time, but in days gone by it was still not exactly a desirable place: it was the site of the town gallows.

Former Chelmsford schoolboy John Dee, who went on to Cambridge University, is said to have studied for eighteen hours a day. He gained his reward, becoming a famous mathematician and astrologer of the sixteenth and early seventeenth centuries.

Many lives on board the *Titanic* were saved thanks to the Marconi Company at Chelmsford. Its wireless equipment had been installed on the doomed ship, not in case there was an emergency, but for the amusement of passengers

Radio has come a long way since the days of Marconi.

who were able to send messages home. However, when the ship hit an iceberg, vessels in the vicinity were able to pick up the radio distress signals.

Few also know that Guglielmo Marconi himself had a return ticket, but was forced to travel to America prior to the voyage due to business.

Also from The History Press

GREAT WAR BRITAIN

Great War Britain is a unique new local series to mark the centenary of the Great War. In partnership with archives and museums across Great Britain, the series provides an evocative portrayal of life during this 'war to end all wars'. In a scrapbook style, and beautifully illustrated, it includes features such as personal memoirs, letters home, diary extracts, newspaper reports, photographs, postcards and other local First World War ephemera.

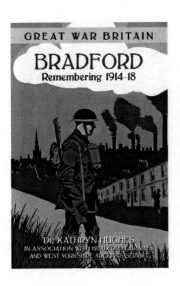

Find these titles and more at
www.thehistorypress.co.uk

Also from The History Press

Ever Wondered What your Town Used to Look Like?

Our *Then & Now* series sets out to illustrate the changing face of the UK's towns and cities in full colour. Contrasting a selection of forty-five archive photographs alongside forty-five modern photographs taken from the same location today, these unique books will compliment every local historian's bookshelf as well as making ideal gifts for everyone interested in knowing more about their hometown.

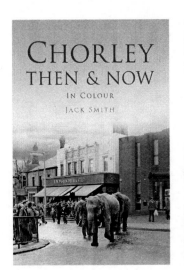

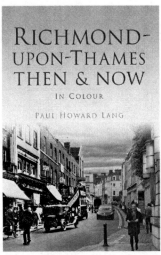

Find these titles and more at
www.thehistorypress.co.uk

Lightning Source UK Ltd.
Milton Keynes UK
UKOW04f0602150714

235136UK00007B/74/P